THREE BODLEY HEAD MONOGRAPHS

GENERAL EDITOR: KATHLEEN LINES

THREE BODLEY HEAD MONOGRAPHS

Lewis Carroll

ROGER LANCELYN GREEN

E. Nesbit

ANTHEA BELL

Howard Pyle

ELIZABETH NESBITT

THE BODLEY HEAD

LONDON SYDNEY

TORONTO

SBN 370 00885 5

Printed and bound in Great Britain for
The Bodley Head Ltd
9 Bow Street, London WC2
by C. Tinling & Co. Ltd, Prescot
Set in Monotype Ehrhardt
First published, in three individual volumes, 1960, 1966
This edition, revised and re-set, 1968

Lewis Carroll

ROGER LANCELYN GREEN

When I came up to Oxford,
  I walked along the High,
And came to Salutation House,
Went in among the books to browse—
  And who so pleased as I!

Full many a ghost I met there
  Who once had walked the High:
A don strolled in from Wonderland
Leading Miss Liddell by the hand—
  I'm sure they passed me by . . .

CONTENTS

1. Youth

The old myths about Lewis Carroll die hard. A recent work on the Child in Literature still talks about him as 'almost the case-book maladjusted neurotic' and dwells on 'Dodgson's frustrated exclusion from life'. Many still believe in the dual personality thesis, 'the strange case of Dr Dodgson and Mr Carroll', invented by Langford Reed over thirty years ago. Even when he is accepted as a more or less normal man of his period, *Alice* comes in for the misplaced ingenuity of the critics instead of its author's supposed fixations, and is demonstrated beneath some new critical microscope as a Freudian Horror Comic, or an allegorical attack on the religious controversies of the day, a veiled page of political history, or even a Judaic cryptogram.

In a sense no man of genius is 'normal', simply because 'genius' is granted only to a few. In the sense that he alone wrote *Alice in Wonderland*, Lewis Carroll is of course unique, and attempts to account for genius lead the searcher into a country even more confusing than that beyond the Looking Glass. But biography can explain the form and background of a work of genius: it can account for the outward and visible body, even if we must still hold that genius, like the soul, 'cometh from afar'.

The background of Charles Lutwidge Dodgson's life and works was a very ordinary and normal one, shared by many another university don of his period—who did not produce an *Alice*.

He was born in the old parsonage at Daresbury in

Cheshire on January 27, 1832, being the third child and eldest son of the Rev. Charles Dodgson (1800-1868) and Frances Jane Lutwidge (1803-1851), who were married at Hull in 1827. Before they left for Croft in 1843, where the youngest, Edwin, was born, Charles had seven sisters and two brothers.

This large family of children was brought up in the very depths of the country, enjoying all the delights of a free, rural life among woods and fields, in farmyards and old-fashioned gardens:

> 'An island farm, 'mid seas of corn,
> Swayed by the wandering breath of morn,
> The happy spot where I was born—'

as Charles was to write of it in 1860 in his poem *Faces in the Fire*.

Only one child from outside the family circle came occasionally to join the children at Daresbury, Vere Bayne, son of the Headmaster of nearby Warrington Grammar School, who became one of Charles's closest friends then and in after-years at Oxford. But, after the fashion of imaginative children, Charles made friends with the smaller denizens of the countryside; even snails, toads and earthworms are recorded—and he is certain to have known more than one Cheshire Cat, even if he never saw the medieval cat at Brimstage who wears a grin on his red stone lips to this day.

One recorded expedition was to Beaumaris in Anglesey, a three-day journey by coach, since the railway did not extend so far. There he explored the great medieval castle with its long passages in the thickness of the ivy-clad walls, and looked down the deep garde-robe pits with their openings at each level—far more like the entrance to that Hall

Underground where the Pool of Tears was to be than any rabbit hole on the low banks of the Isis above Godstow.

The early reading of the Dodgson children is not recorded. Doubtless many books of an improving and religious nature were eked out by the writings of Maria Edgeworth and Harriet Martineau, by *Sandford and Merton* and *Ornaments Discovered*. But fairy tales may have been allowed, and certainly Halliwell-Phillips's collection of *The Nursery Rhymes of England* (1842) (which included 'The Queen of Hearts', 'Humpty-Dumpty', 'Tweedledum and Tweedledee' and 'I love my love with an H'), Edward Lear's first *Book of Nonsense* (1846), and probably Catherine Sinclair's *Holiday House* (1839) with the first example of sheer Nonsense in our literature, 'Uncle David's Non-sensical Story about Giants and Fairies'.

That nonsense was encouraged in Daresbury parsonage is shown by a letter written to Charles at the age of eight by his father:

'. . . I will not forget your commission. As soon as I get to Leeds I shall scream out in the middle of the street, *Ironmongers—Iron*-mongers—Six hundred men will rush out of their shops in a moment—fly, fly, in all directions—ring the bells, call the constables—set the town on fire. I *will* have a file & a screwdriver, & a ring, & if they are not brought directly, in forty seconds I will leave nothing but one small cat alive in the whole town of Leeds, & I shall only leave that, because I am afraid I shall not have time to kill it.'

'To find young Dodgson brought up on parental fantasies of this kind is significant', wrote Derek Hudson, who was first to publish this letter: it is not likely to have been an isolated freak, and we can but wonder how many scraps of his father's nonsense came back to Lewis Carroll years afterwards when he began telling stories to his child-friends.

Meanwhile the Rev. Charles Dodgson was presented to the living of Croft on the borders of Yorkshire and Durham, and the family moved to the big, square Rectory: 'a good old-fashioned rectory', as he described it after his first visit in February 1843, 'with no *beauty* outside or inside, but, as far as I could judge in its state of dismantlement & disorder, possessing the elements of abundant comfort'.

In this new garden Charles began inventing games for his host of brothers and sisters. The favourite was 'The Railway Game', trains being as new and engrossing to a boy of eleven in the eighteen-forties as jet-planes and space-rockets are today. 'He constructed a rude train out of a wheelbarrow, a barrel and a small truck, which used to convey passengers from one "station" in the Rectory garden to another', his nephew tells us. 'At each of these stations] there was a refreshment-room, and the passengers had to purchase tickets from him before they could enjoy their ride.'

Some of his Rules for the Railway Game still survive, and make amusing reading, even when we remember the dangers of real railway travel at that early date:—

I. All passengers when upset are requested to lie still until picked up—as it is requisite that at least 3 trains should go over them, to entitle them to the attention of the doctor and assistants.

II. If a passenger comes up to a station after the train has passed the next (i.e. when it is about 100 m. off) he may not run after it but must wait for the next.

Another amusement was the marionette theatre which [Charles made with the help of the village carpenter and assistance from several of the family. He also wrote plays to be acted in it, the only one of which to survive, *La Guida di Bragia*, turned once again to railways for its inspiration, with Bradshaw himself appearing at the end to declare:

> 'I made a rule my servants were to sing:
> That rule they disobeyed, and in revenge
> I altered all the train times in my book!'

This must have been written about 1845-6 when Charles was beginning to entertain the family with the first of a series of manuscript magazines. *Useful and Instructive Poetry*, composed for his brother Wilfred and his sister Louisa, still exists and has recently been published. In itself it has little value beyond illustrating the mind of an amusing and precocious schoolboy of the period. In the ancestry of *Alice*, however, it has its small place for such fancies as 'A Tale of a Tail' and the story of 'The Headstrong Man' which may be held to foreshadow the Mouse's Tail and the plight of Humpty-Dumpty, though the next effort, *The Rectory Magazine* (finished in 1848), shows the more definite precursors of style and manner. The first 'portmanteau word', for example, occurs in the poem 'Woes' which narrates at rather too great a length how a cannonball found its way down the throat of a lion,

> 'Two chokes, one howl,
> A stifled growl,
> It died without a struggle:
> And the only sound
> That was heard around
> Was its last expiring guggle.'

In the amusing story in prose of 'Crundle Castle', besides the fat and unpleasant boy called 'Guggy', who reappears with a few additional trimmings as Uggug in

Sylvie and Bruno, comes an even more definite use of a 'portmanteau word',

'"I really must show you," began Mrs Cogsby, "a remarkable production of Guggy's. It's a portrait of his father, wonderfully like him, only the poor dear man wouldn't look at it, when I showed it him today, but went off in a fluff." (Probably a combination of flurry and huff, a confusion of words being one of Mrs Cogsby's peculiarities.)'

Meanwhile Charles had joined Richmond Grammar School at the age of twelve, having been grounded excellently in classics and mathematics by his father, and had only happy memories of his two years there under 'my kind old schoolmaster' the Rev. James Tate (1800-63), son of the famous Dr James Tate. He contributed his first story, 'The Unknown One', to the school magazine—a suitable title, since no copy of the periodical in question has survived—and went on to Rugby early in 1846 good at all the necessary subjects of the day except for Latin verse: 'Whether in reading aloud or in metrical composition,' wrote Mr Tate in his last report, he 'frequently sets at naught the notions of Virgil or Ovid as to syllabic quantity. He is moreover marvellously ingenious in replacing the ordinary inflexions of nouns and verbs, as detailed in our grammars, by more exact analogies, or convenient forms of his own devising.'

In consequence Charles wasted much of his time at Rugby in writing impositions, and heartily disliked in retrospect his time at the school. 'I cannot say that I look back upon my life at a Public School with any sensations of pleasure,' he wrote many years later, 'or that any earthly considerations would induce me to go through my three

[sic] years again.' Although there is no record of direct bullying, Charles noted his sufferings as a new boy from the older boys robbing their juniors of bedclothes at night in the big open dormitories. He took little interest in games, preferring long walks in the country, and was eager to read new books whenever possible and write at length about them to one or other of his sisters.

He left Rugby at the end of 1849 after four years, and at once began another magazine, *The Rectory Umbrella*, for the family at Croft, which shows a considerable advance on his earlier work. Foreshadowings of *Alice* may be found in the 'Zoological Paper' on the Lory, and of the Professor's experiment in *Sylvie and Bruno* in a footnote to an amusing story 'The Walking-Stick of Destiny' which reads: 'It is difficult to imagine what black light can look like. It may be obtained by pouring ink over a candle in a dark-room.' But the real advance is in technical ability and in the art of parody, exemplified by the 'Lay of Sorrow' in the style of 'Horatius'.

The year 1850 was spent by Charles Dodgson at Croft, studying with his father (by now Archdeacon of Ripon) for his entry to Christ Church, Oxford. He matriculated on May 23 of that year, but, as was common at the time, there was no place for him in the college until the following January.

His first term had scarcely begun when he was summoned home by the sudden death of his mother, a blow which meant more to him than is readily apparent. Writing many years later to his sister Mary on the birth of the son who lived to become his first biographer, Charles Dodgson ended, 'May you be to him what our own dear mother was to *her* eldest son. I can hardly utter for your boy a better wish than that.'

Every scrap of evidence points to Dodgson's exceedingly happy childhood, apart from his dislike of his public school, and of his devotion to both his parents. There is no suggestion of conflict with his father or of the slightest repression by him, in spite of attempts which have been made to explain Lewis Carroll by means of his supposed failure in the Freudian attempt to 'surpass his parents—if this seems hopeless', the theory goes, 'he may give up, and twist himself into perverse patterns'.

As a corrective to this way of thinking it is of interest to consider C. S. Lewis's analysis of the character of George MacDonald, Dodgson's contemporary and friend:

'We have learned from Freud and others about those distortions in character and errors in thought which result from a man's early conflicts with his father. Far the most important thing that we can know about George Mac-Donald is that his whole life illustrates the opposite process. An almost perfect relationship with his father was the earthly root of all his wisdom. From his own father, he said, he first learned that Fatherhood must be at the core of the universe. He was thus prepared in an unusual way to teach that religion in which the relation of Father and Son is of all relations the most central.'

As in the case of MacDonald, Dodgson found no cause, even while crossing the troublesome years between youth and manhood, to doubt the truth of the Christian revelation. He was brought up in a religious household, with morning and evening prayers and two visits to church every Sunday; at Christ Church he found religion, in the afterglow of the Oxford Movement, very much a subject for vital discussion —but still held by the majority of thinking men. With his background, he came naturally to accept the clear middle course prescribed by the ordinary Church of England training; no 'reaction' against authority, parental or otherwise, caused him to fly into the extremes of the Evangelical or Roman persuasions—nor, as with many of the weaker brethren, to break away into the desperate paths of Agnosticism impelled by the dubious findings of Charles Darwin, and the incendiary teachings of Huxley and Tyndall.

No doubt came his way, save of his own unworthiness; the strictest studies in logic served only to strengthen his faith, as the interesting 'Letter to an Agnostic', written in the last year of his life, and first published in the Appendix to his *Diaries* (1953) amply proves. Indeed age, thought and experience tended only, while strengthening his faith, to lower the artificial barriers over which Newman and Pusey had wasted so much energy. In 1890 he wrote to a friend,

'More and more I am becoming content to know that Christians have *many* ways of looking at their religion, and less confident that my views must be right and all others wrong, and less anxious to bring everybody to think as I do.'

Indeed, when a young friend who had recently been received into the Church of Rome visited him at Oxford a few years before his death, he accompanied her to Mass at St Aloysius, and grieved over the narrowness of her spiritual adviser who would not allow her to accompany him to the University Sermon at St Mary's.

II. Oxford

When Dodgson came up to Christ Church in January 1851, to remain there (though he did not yet know it) for the rest of his life, it was to an Oxford very different from that of today. The place itself was still the little medieval University town, with a few imposing buildings of the eighteenth century and occasional 'Gothic' additions made to beautify ancient buildings to the eyes of Regency dons. 'On all sides except where it touched the railway,' wrote Edward Burne Jones, two years Dodgson's junior, 'the city ended abruptly, as if a wall had been about it, and you came suddenly upon the meadows. There was little brick in the city, it was either grey with stone or yellow with the wash of the pebble-dash in the poorer streets.' Members of the University, old and young, wore caps and gowns as they hurried about the streets, and were so much the main inhabitants that grass did actually grow up between the cobbles of the deserted High during the Long Vacation.

Life in the colleges was undergoing a transition. Though teaching in the main was still restricted to theology, classics and mathematics, a new spirit and a new eagerness for learning were abroad. The complacent don sinking into ignorant dotage over his port was fast giving place under the stimulus of dedicated teachers like Newman and Pusey, Mark Pattison and Jowett, to the eager tutor or lecturer earnest in the cause of learning, ambitious for his pupils and proud of the corporate achievements of his college.

The 'Gentleman Commoner', who hunted three days a week and passed his time, after the bare minimum of two hours' work a day, in drinking, gaming and wenching, was fast dying out, though still accentuated in such works of fiction as *Tom Brown at Oxford* and *The Adventures of Mr Verdant Green*. When Dodgson arrived at Christ Church 'the position of the undergraduates was much more similar to that of schoolboys. They were subject to the same penalties . . . , and were expected to work, and to work hard.'

This suited Dodgson ideally. He had always had an enthusiasm for work, his particular bent being mathematics, and he was of a shy and retiring disposition, shunning rowdy parties and any excessive absorption in the trivialities of sport, while his strict moral sense, and his knowledge of his duty to remain within the narrow allowance which was all that his father could afford to make him, kept him from the temptations and frivolities of the 'smarter' sets.

In short, he worked hard and conscientiously at Oxford, with an academic career as his goal; in 1851 he gained a Boulter Scholarship; at the end of the following year he won First Class Honours in Mathematical and Second in Classical Moderations, and was elected by Dr Pusey to a Studentship—the equivalent of a Fellowship in other colleges.

Early in the summer of 1854, after working as much as thirteen hours a day for the last few weeks, he took his final examination in classics, but only achieved Third Class Honours. During a few weeks of less strenuous work that summer he contributed his first poems to the public press, two sets of quite undistinguished serious verse to *Hall's Oxonian Advertiser*; and while on a reading holiday in Whitby that August and September, a story, and some really amusing verses called 'The Lady of the Ladle' to *The Whitby Gazette*.

During this same visit to Whitby one of the other men

reading with him remembered afterwards how he had sat on the shore telling stories to children which were, he felt, the first germs of *Alice in Wonderland*. No trace of these early stories remains, but from the summer of 1854 date the nonsense verses which afterwards became the 'Evidence' read by the White Rabbit at the trial of the Knave of Hearts.

Back in Oxford, Dodgson set to work again for the Final Mathematical School, in which he obtained First Class Honours, and took his B.A. on December 18. After this he settled down to the life of an Oxford don; for the first part of 1855 he was merely tutoring a small number of private pupils, and earning a little extra money as Sub-Librarian (a position he held for less than two years). But in the autumn of 1855 he was appointed Mathematical Lecturer of Christ Church, the equivalent of the modern College Tutor, and with this his future was assured, so that he could write on the last day of the year that 'It has been the most eventful year of my life: I began it as a poor Bachelor Student, with no definite plans or expectations; I end it as a Master and Tutor in Christ Church, with an income of more than £300 a year, and a course of mathematical tuition marked out by God's providence for at least some years to come.'

When becoming a Student of Christ Church, Dodgson had undertaken as part of his qualification for the position that he would remain unmarried and proceed to ordination at the usual age. He was ordained a deacon on December 22, 1861, but did not proceed to take priest's orders, holding himself unfit for parochial work. The choice lay open to him; had he wished to marry and proceed to full ordination, he would have forfeited his Studentship, but Christ Church would have preferred him to one of the college livings—a future which he certainly had in view in 1855.

By 1860, however, 'I found myself established as the Mathematical Lecturer, and with no sort of inclination to give it up and take parochial work.' He came to the conclusion 'that, so far from educational work (even mathematics) being unfit occupation for a clergyman, it was distinctly a *good* thing that many of our educators should be men in Holy Orders'. Besides his unfitness for parochial duties, Dodgson felt himself more suited for other kinds of work, and he did not proceed to priest's orders partly because he felt that had he done so he might find it his duty to take a parish, but also because the strict outlook among bishops at the time would have made it necessary for him to give up his ardent theatre-going, and perhaps even his lighter literary work and his photography.

From early years Dodgson had been interested in art and eager to become an artist, at least in black and white. All the family magazines were copiously illustrated by him, and it was only when his humorous drawings were refused by *The Comic Times* in 1855 that he reluctantly let his dreams of artistic success lapse in favour of literature.

Perhaps as a compensation for this deprivation, he began to interest himself in the new art of photography in the following year, and soon purchased a camera and set to work with enthusiasm on the difficult task of taking time-exposures on glass plates coated with collodion which needed to be developed immediately.

'It is my one recreation,' he wrote in his diary at the end of 1856, 'and I think that it should be done well.'

This new interest was reflected in his literary work. His last contribution to *The Comic Times* was the story 'Photography Extraordinary', and in December 1857 his best known photographic verses, 'Hiawatha's Photographing', appeared in *The Train*, for which he had begun to write.

In pursuit of his new hobby, Dodgson visited several well-known people of the day and took photographs of Tennyson and his family, the Rossettis ('once the author of *Wonderland* photographed us in the garden,' recorded Christina), Ruskin, Charlotte Yonge, Mrs Craik, Millais and his children, the George MacDonalds, Ellen Terry and her sisters, and many statesmen, churchmen and professors.

But it was with children that Dodgson obtained his best results, and many a child-friend records the thrilling hours spent in his little studio on the roof above his rooms at Christ Church where they would be posed in different positions and various costumes—afterwards attending in wide-eyed wonder at the 'mystic, awful' process of developing the picture on the glass plate.

In 1949 Mr Helmut Gernsheim, the great historian of photography, published sixty-four of Dodgson's best pictures in his book *Lewis Carroll—Photographer*, and wrote that 'his photographic achievements are truly astonishing; he must not only rank as a pioneer of British amateur photography, but I would also unhesitatingly acclaim him as the most outstanding photographer of children in the nineteenth century.' For his pictures of adults, 'after Julia Margaret Cameron he is probably the most distinguished amateur portraitist of the mid-Victorian era. . . . He was a master of composition, which was one of Mrs Cameron's weak points.' It may be added that Dodgson was one of the only three British photographers to be included in the famous 'Family of Man' exhibition in 1956, the other two being contemporary artists using the most modern cameras and apparatus.

Photographing Ellen Terry raises the question of the one possible romance of Lewis Carroll's life. Collingwood, his nephew and first biographer, hinted that a disappointment shadowed his uncle's life, and inspired some of the poems of unrequited love which were written mainly in the early 'sixties and collected in *Three Sunsets*. 'He was as fond of me as he could be of anyone over the age of ten,' she wrote, 'I can't remember when I didn't know him.' Dodgson's eldest sister, Frances, believed, as Collingwood wrote in a private letter in 1932, 'that Uncle Charles had had a disappointment in love and . . . that the lady in question was Ellen Terry. When Ellen Terry was just growing up— about 17—she was lovely beyond description . . . and it is highly probable that he fell in love with her.' Collingwood thought that Dodgson might even have proposed to Ellen Terry, but this is certainly untrue, since at the time when he met her and, presumably 'fell' for her, she was married to G. F. Watts, even though living apart from him. Dodgson may perhaps have fallen in love; with his rigid standard of Christian morality he cannot even have considered proposing to her—quite apart from his habitual shyness which would have made this difficult, even in more legitimate circumstances, and the preposterous idea (for those days) of a clergyman marrying an actress.

The vain love, the disappointment, the shadow (though there is no hint of any of them in his diaries) may have come to Lewis Carroll when he first met Ellen Terry in December 1864. But it seems certain that there were no other lost loves, and that he never considered marriage as a serious possibility with a particular girl in mind.

Perhaps the most important difference between Lewis Carroll and the majority of mankind was the affliction which was upon him all his life—his incurable stammer. Several sisters and one brother shared this to a lesser degree, and it has been suggested that in-breeding was in part at least the cause of it, since his parents were first cousins.

The statement that Dodgson was naturally left-handed but forced to use his right hand, though made by several writers on Lewis Carroll, is quite without foundation.

Whatever the cause, Dodgson grew up with this affliction. In the home circle it was taken for granted, and did not disturb him; but what he must have suffered at Rugby, though he makes no allusion to this particular trouble, can only be understood by those who have shared his disability.

Stammering brings with it extreme reserve, shyness and awkwardness. In excitement an occasional outburst lets loose a torrent of words in which far more is said than is meant—'as wine comes out of a narrow-mouth'd bottle,—either too much at once, or none at all'; Shakespeare has the perfect description. Stammering is apt to set a young man apart from his fellows; though they may not jeer, he feels that they pity or endure him—and the stammer becomes worse immediately. This goes far to explain Dodgson's aloofness at Oxford, his preference for quiet study by himself, the fact that he never got drawn into the religious and political controversies which were sweeping Oxford in the 'fifties and 'sixties; that he stood outside, and took part only with his pen, and usually on subjects of a secular nature where light-hearted banter and humorous satire might suitably be employed. *Notes by an Oxford Chiel* and his other amusing comments in prose and verse on matters of University interest never touch on religion. That the *Alice* books are basically religious satire, as Mr A. L. Taylor suggests in *The White Knight* (1952) and Dr Abraham Ettleson in his '*Through the Looking-Glass' Decoded* (1966), is quite unthinkable; when a friend pointed out to Dodgson that the passion flower had a religious significance, he substituted a tiger lily immediately, and he was greatly upset by critics who likened the end of *Through the Looking-Glass* to a passage in

Pilgrim's Progress and pointed out that ' 'Tis the voice of the lobster' might be considered irreverent because it parodied a poem which was itself based on certain verses in the *Book of Proverbs*.

If Dodgson felt awkward and uncomfortable in the society of his male contemporaries, he found himself even more at a disadvantage in the presence of that terrifying creature, a young woman of marriageable age. Flirtation was unthinkable; an arch remark would have tied him in literal knots to get out one word, and it is not surprising that he avoided dances and Commemoration Balls like the plague—though he could joke over his refusal to participate.

'As to dancing, my dear,' he wrote to Gaynor Simpson in 1873, 'I *never* dance, unless I am allowed to do it in *my own peculiar way*. There is no use trying to describe it; it has to be seen to be believed. The last house I tried it in, the floor broke through. But then it was a poor sort of floor—the beams were only six inches thick, hardly worth calling beams at all; stone arches are much more sensible, when any dancing, *of my peculiar kind*, is to be done. . . .'

Or, at a much earlier date, when excusing himself from accompanying some young friends to an Oxford Commemoration,

'Yet what are all such gaieties to me
  Whose thoughts are full of indices and surds?

$$x^2 + 7x + 53$$
$$= \frac{11}{3}.$$

If Dodgson could have become an actor he might have overcome his stammer, for many stammerers can act without the slightest hesitation, and the confidence so born soon flows over into ordinary life. Perhaps, subconsciously, he realised this and it added to the fascination which the theatre always held for him; certainly, though his pupils did not realise it, he was forced to act at their lectures and classes, and 'the singularly dry and perfunctory manner in which he imparted instruction to us, never betraying the slightest personal interest in matters that were of deep concern to us', was the rôle he assumed to enable him to lecture at all.

He found school-teaching similarly difficult when he attempted it in 1856 as a part-time master at St Aldates School, Oxford, was unable to maintain discipline, and soon gave up, his distaste for boys being increased by the experience.

His fondness for children in general and small girls in particular, however, grew and increased with the years. Not only from his experiences as organiser of family games and stories at Daresbury and Croft, was he accustomed to the society of children, but with them alone he did not stammer. The difficulties of adult intercourse caused a certain amount of nostalgia for his childhood, and though he was thinking of his dead mother when he wrote the poem 'Solitude' in March 1853, this nostalgia was also breaking out in the last stanza,

> 'I'd give all wealth that years have piled,
> The slow result of Life's decay,
> To be once more a little child
> For one bright summer-day.'

There is no suggestion of a Peter Pan complex in this, nor any unusual morbidity. That it is the natural reaction of the stammerer who is only free from his handicap when mixing on terms as equal as possible with children seems to be confirmed by another writer similarly handicapped and finding relief in the same outlet, who wrote at precisely the same age,

> 'If love be but a dream, why then
> This truth I'd have you know:
> I would I were a child again,
> With thee as playfellow.'

That there was a 'Mr Carroll' as distinct from 'Mr Dodgson' in this one respect is well shown by the recollections of a child-friend of his later years, Isa Bowman. Dodgson took her to see the static 'panorama' of the Niagara Falls, and proceeded to tell her whimsical stories about the dog in the foreground 'which, he said, was really alive but trained to stand motionless for hours'; and he

'... added other absurd details about the dog, how, if we waited long enough, we should see an attendant bring him a bone, how he was allowed so many hours off each day when his brother, who unfortunately was rather restless, would take his place, and how this badly behaved animal on one occasion jumped right out of the panorama among the onlookers, attracted by the sight of a little girl's sandwich, and so on. Suddenly he began to stammer and looking round in some alarm, I saw that a dozen grown-ups and children had gathered around and were listening with every appearance of amused interest. And it was not Mr Carroll but a very confused Mr Dodgson who took me by the hand and led me quickly from the scene.'

The glorious freedom from the stammer and all that goes with it which he found in the society of children led Dodgson, as others who have discovered the same means of release can well appreciate, to spend more and more of his time with children and give freer and freer reign to that side of his imagination which could produce the fantastic verses and the prosaically nonsensical stories in which most children delight.

The Rectory Umbrella was more or less finished by the time he went up to Oxford, but he was still an undergraduate in August 1854 when his friend Thomas Fowler remembered how at Whitby 'Dodgson used to sit on a rock on the beach, telling stories to a circle of eager young listeners of both sexes'; and the following year he began *Mischmasch*, the last of the family magazines, by copying in his delightful parody of the Border Ballad style 'The Two Brothers'.

The next entry, 'Poetry for the Million', appeared in *The Comic Times*, and thereafter most of the items in *Mischmasch* were either cuttings pasted into the volume, or sets of verses which subsequently appeared in such periodicals as *The Train*, *The Oxford Critic* or *College Rhymes*.

The items in *The Comic Times* were anonymous, but the first of Dodgson's contributions to *The Train*, the serious poem 'Solitude' published in the number for March 1856, bore the famous pseudonym, made by translating Charles Lutwidge into Latin as Carolus Ludovicus, reversing the order and re-translating as Lewis Carroll. Thereafter all his non-academic writings were published under this name, for he was soon to begin the series of works by 'Charles L. Dodgson' such as *A Syllabus of Plain Algebraical Geometry* (1860), *Condensation of Determinants* (1866) and *Euclid and his Modern Rivals* (1879). An occasional pamphlet, and his satires on Oxford affairs appeared anonymously or as by 'D.C.L.' who, indeed, appears in one of them as 'Mr de Ciel'.

But, if we wish to make the distinction, the career of Lewis Carroll, entertainer of children other than his own brothers and sisters, began at about the same time that he adopted his *nom-de-plume*. The first extant volume of his

Diary, that for 1855, shows him already making friends with children at the seaside, with the three Crawshay children at Tynemouth in August, and later the same month with Frederica Liddell, the niece of the new Dean of Christ Church, at Whitburn, 'one of the most lovely children I ever saw, gentle and innocent looking, not an inanimate doll-beauty', and her sister Gertrude. On September 21, while walking on the shore he 'fell in with my favourite little Liddells', and spent about an hour with them, 'story-telling, etc.'

These are the first of many references in his *Diaries* to the child-friends who, by the end of his life, ran literally into hundreds. To them he told stories and wrote nonsense letters and verse acrostics; he took them to the theatre, entertained them in London, at Oxford or at Eastbourne where he usually spent a couple of months each summer: 'I cannot understand how anyone could be bored by little children,' he confessed about 1890, 'they are three-fourths of my life.'

Dodgson was already writing amusing nonsense letters to his own family at least as early as 1855. To some of his earliest child-friends, the children of George MacDonald, he wrote not long afterwards letters containing such delicious foreshadowings of his *Alice* manner as,

'Don't be in such a hurry to believe next time—I'll tell you why—If you set to work to believe everything you will tire out the muscles of your mind, and then you'll be so weak you won't be able to believe the simplest true things. Only last week a friend of mine set to work to believe Jack-the-giant-killer. He managed to do it, but he was so exhausted by it that when I told him it was raining (which was true) he *couldn't* believe it, but rushed out into the street without his hat or umbrella. . . .

'Now I want to know what you *mean* by calling yourself "naughty" for not having written sooner! Naughty, indeed! Stuff and nonsense! Do you think *I'd* call myself naughty if I hadn't written to you, say, for 50 years? Not a bit! I'd just begin as usual "My dear Mary, 50 years ago you asked me what to do for your kitten, as it had a tooth-ache, and I have just remembered to write about it. Perhaps the tooth-ache has gone off by this time—if not, wash it carefully in hasty-pudding, and give it 4 pin cushions boiled in sealing-wax, and just dip the end of its tail in hot coffee. This remedy has never been known to fail." There! *That's* the proper way to write!'

It is certainly the proper way to write for children, and doubtless Alice Liddell and her sisters received numerous letters even more amusing than these, if only they had survived—and were taught, like the White Queen, to believe 'as many as six impossible things before breakfast!'

III. Alice

Dodgson first met Alice on April 25, 1856, just before her fourth birthday when he was visiting the Deanery at Christ Church to take a photograph of the Cathedral; 'The three little girls were in the garden most of the time, and we became excellent friends.' Lorina the eldest was seven at this time, and Edith was two, while their brother Harry whom Dodgson had already met and was to tutor for a little while was nine. The friendship grew and continued for almost ten years, though Dodgson never got on well with either the Dean or Mrs Liddell; he seldom visited at the Deanery, except to see the children, and he certainly never stayed with the Liddells at Llandudno, as legend has it that he did. Entries in his diary show that his visits to the Deanery were usually timed to coincide with Mrs Liddell's absence from home. The children, however, visited him in his rooms fairly frequently, sometimes accompanied by their governess Miss Prickett, who was nicknamed 'Pricks', and who may have been the original of the Mouse in *Wonderland*, since the history lesson beginning: 'William the Conqueror whose cause was favoured by the Pope . . .' is an actual quotation from Havilland Chepmell's *Short Course of History* (1862), pages 143-4, which was one of their lesson-books.

Dodgson told many stories to the three little girls before the famous picnic which produced the main part of *Alice in Wonderland*:

'We used to sit on the big sofa on each side of him,' remembered Alice in 1932, 'while he told us stories, illustrating them by pencil or ink drawings as he went

31

along. . . . He seemed to have an endless store of these fantastical tales, which he made up as he told them, drawing busily on a large sheet of paper all the time. They were not always entirely new. Sometimes they were new versions of old stories; sometimes they started on the old basis, but grew into new tales owing to the frequent interruptions which opened up fresh and undreamed of possibilities.'

Among these stories was 'A Mad Tea Party', in which the three children appear as the little girls who lived in the treacle well, Elsie being 'L.C.' (Lorina Charlotte), Lacie an anagram of 'Alice' and Tilly being short for 'Matilda' which was Edith's nickname. 'Pig and Pepper' may also have been one of these stories, since Cheshire Cats were in Dodgson's mind at the time, following a correspondence in *Notes and Queries* (of which he was an eager reader) on the origin of the expression 'To grin like a Cheshire Cat'. He must have followed with amusement the various old—and odd—explanations unearthed by the learned in their vain attempts to explain the phrase. Do Cheshire Cats grin because Cheshire is the only County Palatine? Or were snarling armorial leopards (of which the Red Cat of Brimstage may be one) painted on so many inn signs in Cheshire made more like grinning cats by painters who had never seen a leopard? Or was Cheshire cheese made into the shape of a cat before being sent for export to Bristol? Or was it simply that the young ladies of Cheshire (referred to as 'The Cheshire Cats' by their cousins in the next county, 'The Lancashire Witches') were noted for the breadth of their smiles?

Dodgson did not enter into the controversy, but he noted that it was not getting anywhere.

'"Would you tell me please, which way I ought to go from here?"

"That depends a good deal on where you want to get to," said the Cat.

"I don't much care where," said Alice.

"Then it doesn't matter which way you go," said the Cat.

"—So long as I get somewhere," Alice added as an explanation.

"Oh, you're sure to do that," said the Cat, "if you only walk long enough."

Alice felt that this could not be denied . . .'

The Cheshire Cat correspondence having faded away, leaving only the grin—still unaccounted for—Dodgson, with a passing thought for an even older phrase 'A cat may look at a king', was ready to begin wondering how 'As mad as a hatter' originated. The tea-party may have been a fairly mad one in Dodgson's rooms when, according to Alice, he would say, 'Now then, it's a rainy day, let's have some tea.' Ordinary afternoon tea had not yet come into fashion, but Dodgson's suggestion would be timed to coincide with the children's 'tea' at 6 p.m.—hence the hour at which the Mad Hatter's watch had stopped. When Miss Prickett was not available, the children were escorted by their nurse who, we can well imagine, was apt to drop off to sleep like any Dormouse.

'When we went on the river for the afternoon with Mr Dodgson,' recorded Alice, 'which happened at most four or five times every summer term, he always brought out with him a large basket full of cakes, and a kettle, which we used to boil under a haycock, if we could find one. On rarer occasions we went out for the whole day with him, and then we took a large basket with luncheon—cold chicken and salad and all sorts of good things. One of our favourite whole-day excursions was to row down to Nuneham and picnic in the woods there. . . .

'The party usually consisted of five—one of Mr Dodg-son's men friends as well as himself and us three. His brother [Wilfred] occasionally took an oar in the merry party, but our most usual fifth was Mr Duckworth, who sang well. . . .'

On June 17, 1862 an important expedition took place. Dodgson's two eldest sisters, Fanny and Elizabeth, and his Aunt Lucy Lutwidge were staying in Oxford as his guests, and he took them on an all-day picnic on the river, with Robinson Duckworth, who was then a young don at Trinity, to help him row, 'Ina, Alice and Edith came with us'. They set out at twelve-thirty, got to Nuneham by two, and landed there to have dinner and walk in the park, before starting back at half past four. 'About a mile above Nuneham heavy rain came on', recorded Dodgson in his diary.

'After bearing it for a short time I settled that we had better leave the boat and walk; three miles of this drenched us all pretty well. I went on first with the children as they could walk much faster than Elizabeth, and took them to the only house I knew in Sandford, Mrs Broughton's, where Ranken lodges. I left them with her to get their clothes dried, and went off to find a vehicle. . . . We all had tea in my rooms about 8.30, after which I took the children home.'

Just over a fortnight later, Dodgson and Duckworth took the three children on another river expedition, upstream this time, and for the afternoon only. It was on July 4, and is probably the most famous picnic that has ever taken place. 'Duckworth and I made an expedition *up* the river to Godstow with the three Liddells; we had tea on the bank there, and did not reach Christ Church again till quarter past eight. . . . On which occasion,' he added later, 'I told them the fairy-tale of *Alice's Adventures Underground*, which I undertook to write out for Alice.'

34

'The story was actually composed and spoken *over my shoulder* for the benefit of Alice Liddell,' wrote Duckworth. 'I remember turning round and saying, "Dodgson, is this an extemporary romance of yours?" And he replied: "Yes, I'm inventing as we go along." I also remember how, when we had conducted the three children back to the Deanery, Alice said, as she bade us good-night, "Oh, Mr Dodgson, I wish you would write out Alice's Adventures for me!" . . .'

And Alice Liddell recorded, 'I think the stories he told us that afternoon must have been better than usual, because I have such a distinct recollection of the expedition, and also, on the next day I started to pester him to write down the story for me.'

On the next day, sure enough, Dodgson records that he set out for London and by chance travelled with the Liddells, and he added, concerning the story, 'Headings written out on my way to London.'

And the story itself? 'I distinctly remember,' wrote Dodgson, 'how, in a desperate attempt to strike out some new line in fairy-lore, I had sent my heroine straight down a rabbit-hole, to begin with, without the least idea what was to happen afterwards.'

Having got Alice down into the hall underground, Dodgson harked back to the disastrous expedition to Nuneham of two weeks previous—when, as likely as not, Alice, in the midst of their discomforts, had burst into tears and been accused of causing the flood by her crying, while one of the party may have remarked that it was 'raining cats and dogs', at which odd expression the children might have protested that if so they hated cats and dogs.

'They were indeed a curious party that assembled on the bank,' wrote Dodgson in his original version, 'the birds with draggled feathers, the animals with their fur clinging close to them—all dripping wet, cross and uncomfortable. The first question of course was how to get dry: they had a consultation about this, and Alice hardly felt herself at all surprised at finding herself talking familiarly with the birds, as if she had known them all her life. Indeed, she had quite a long argument with the Lory, who at last turned sulky, and would only say "I am older than you, and must know best", and this Alice would not admit without knowing how old the Lory was, and as the Lory positively refused to tell its age, there was nothing more to be said.'

After this, the Mouse gave its history lesson; but even Havilland Chepmell did not prove dry enough for the purpose.

'"In that case," said the Dodo solemnly, rising to his feet, "I move that the meeting adjourn, for the immediate adoption of more energetic remedies—"

"Speak English!" said the Duck. "I don't know the meaning of half those long words, and what's more, I don't believe you do either!" And the Duck quacked a comfortable laugh to itself. Some of the other birds tittered audibly.

"I only meant to say," said the Dodo in rather an offended tone, "that I know of a house near here, where we could get the young lady and the rest of the party dried, and then we could listen comfortably to the story which I think you were good enough to promise to tell us," bowing gravely to the Mouse.

'The Mouse made no objection to this, and the whole party moved along the river bank (for the pool had by this time begun to flow out of the hall, and the edge of it was fringed with rushes and forget-me-nots) in a slow procession, the Dodo leading the way. After a time the Dodo became impatient, and, leaving the Duck to bring up the rest of the party, moved on at a quicker pace with Alice, the

Lory and the Eaglet, and soon brought them to a little cottage, and there they sat snugly by the fire, wrapped up in blankets, until the rest of the party had arrived, and they were all dry again.'

After this the Mouse proceeded with its tale—' "It *is* a long tail, certainly," said Alice, looking down with wonder at the mouse's tail, which was coiled nearly all round the party.' (Was Dodgson remembering his early poem—'It was a tail of desperate length'—or was Aunt Lucy Lutwidge wearing so long a boa that she had wrapped it round the three children when the rain began?)

The 'Tale' was different from the final one which tells what 'Fury said to a mouse', but after it Alice made the same injudicious remarks about Dinah—the tabby cat at the Deanery, 'my special pet'—and when she was left alone, she

'began talking to herself again as usual, "I do wish some of them had stayed a little longer! and I was getting to be such friends with them—really the Lory and I were almost like sisters! and so was the dear little Eaglet! And then the Duck and the Dodo! How nicely the Duck sang to us as we came along through the water; and if the Dodo hadn't known the way to that nice little cottage, I don't know when we should have got dry again. . . ." '

The fun of the story was increased by the realisation that the Lory was Lorina and the Eaglet was Edith, while Dodgson ('Do-do-dodgson' when he stammered) was the Dodo and Duckworth was the Duck, 'The Duck from the Dodo', wrote Dodgson in the copy of the facsimile of *Alice's Adventures Underground* which he gave to Duckworth in 1887.

Duckworth's songs were a great feature of the expeditions

and the children learnt to sing 'Sally come up', the nigger minstrel song by T. Ramsey and E. W. Mackney which was parodied in the story,

> 'Salmon come up! Salmon go down!
> Salmon come twist your tail around . . .'

And not long afterwards Dodgson visited them at the Deanery to write in the books for collections of crests (including their own which sported 'Three leopards' faces, or'—the Cheshire Cat of heraldry; and probably the Gryphon of Wales, as well as the Lion and the Unicorn in the Royal coat of arms) he listened to them singing J. M. Sayles's 'Beautiful Star',

> 'Beautiful star in heav'n so bright
> Softly falls thy silv'ry light,
> As thou movest from earth so far,
> Star of the evening, beautiful star,
>   Beau-ti-ful star,
>   Beau-ti-ful star,
> Star of the eve-ning,
>   Beautiful, beautiful star.'

This became 'Beautiful Soup' very readily, after the Gryphon and the Mock Turtle had danced the Lobster Quadrille while singing 'Salmon come up!' But between these two adventures Alice had twice tried to recite the poems which Miss Prickett taught them in the school-room: 'How doth the little busy bee', by Isaac Watts, and Robert Southey's 'You are old, father William', both of which suffered a Wonderland change in the process.

Even the story as first written down was not all told on July 4, for on August 6 Dodgson wrote in his diary,

'In the afternoon Harcourt and I took the three Liddells up to Godstow, where we had tea; we tried the game of

"The Ural Mountains" on the way, but it did not prove very successful, and I had to go on with my interminable fairy-tale of *Alice's Adventures*. We got back soon after eight, and had supper in my rooms, the children coming over for a short while. A very enjoyable expedition—the last, I should think, to which Ina is likely to be allowed to come—her fourteenth time.'

It was certainly the last expedition that year, for the Liddells went off next day to their summer home at Llandudno. On November 13 Dodgson 'began writing the fairy tale for Alice, which I told them July 4, going to Godstow—I hope to finish it by Christmas'. But it was not actually finished until early in February 1863, and he was not able to finish the illustrations in the beautifully written copy for Alice until September of the year after.

The story without pictures, however, was to be seen at the Deanery in 1863, and there one day the novelist Henry Kingsley who was visiting the Dean chanced to pick it up, and once started could not lay it down until he had finished. He urged Mrs Liddell to persuade the author to publish it; but Dodgson was doubtful, and did not want to risk losing money over it. However he consulted Duckworth, who read what had been written, and assured him that the book would succeed, if only he could persuade some good artist to illustrate it, and suggested John Tenniel who drew excellent cartoons of animals in *Punch*, and had recently illustrated *Aesop's Fables*.

Dodgson, however, was still uncertain whether a story composed extempory for three particular children, and based moreover on their own experiences, from picnics on the Thames to unusual games of croquet and cards at the Deanery (he had the rules for his new *Court Circular* printed in 1860, and for *Croquet Castles* in 1863), could appeal to other children. As a final test he lent the story (probably in his own rough copy) to George MacDonald who had already written several delightful fairy tales such as 'The Light Princess'. MacDonald took it home and his wife read it out loud to the children. 'I remember that first reading well,' wrote Greville MacDonald in his *Reminiscences of a Specialist* in 1932, 'and also my braggart avowal that I wished there were 60,000 volumes of it.' If Greville, aged six, could be so enthusiastic, and such an expert as George MacDonald advocated publication, Dodgson could hesitate no longer, and he at once set about revising and enlarging the story to make it more suitable for publication.

Out came the more definite references to the picnic at Nuneham, and also Alice's slighting references to Gertrude and Florence (probably friends or cousins of her own) to be replaced by 'Ada' and 'Mabel' who could not be identified. The Caucus Race was substituted for the warm fire and blankets at Sandford and a better tail was given to the Mouse; the Gryphon and the Mock Turtle discoursed at far greater length on the education of the young—though all their 'extras' still paralleled those which, in default of Miss Prickett, Alice received from outside instructors: the Drawing-master, though hardly 'an old conger-eel'—he was actually John Ruskin—did come once a week to teach Drawing, Sketching and Painting in Oils. Instead of 'Salmon come up', the Mock Turtle sang a parody of 'Will you walk into my parlour, said the spider to the fly', and Alice was given another recitation meant to be Isaac Watts's ' 'Tis the voice of the sluggard, I heard him complain, "You have waked me too soon, I must slumber again." ' At this time Dodgson only gave her four lines for the first stanza, and for the second merely,

'I passed by his garden and marked with one eye
How the owl and the oyster were sharing a pie—'

When the songs were set to music in 1870 by William Boyd, Dodgson added two more lines,

'While the Duck and the Dodo, the Lizard and Cat
Were swimming in milk round the brim of a hat.'

It was not until 1886 when *Alice* was made into an operetta that he wrote the sixteen-line version now generally known, with the last complete line (only cut in the book because the Mock Turtle must still interrupt),

'And concluded the banquet by eating the Owl.'

The most important additions, however, were the chapters called 'Pig and Pepper' and 'A Mad Tea Party', 'Who Stole the Tarts?' and 'Alice's Evidence'. There was no Duchess in *Alice's Adventures Underground*: the White Rabbit exclaimed, 'The Marchioness! the Marchioness! Oh my dear paws! oh my fur and whiskers! She'll have me executed, as sure as ferrets are ferrets!', which was rather awkwardly tacked on to what must have been another story, built up round Dodgson's card game of *Court Circular* by letting him tell Alice: 'The Queen's the Marchioness, didn't you know that?'

The Cook, the Cat and the Mad Tea Party were waiting to be fitted in from another story, introduced by the Fish Footmen—perhaps suggested by a 'learned' article on talking fish, with an amusing du Maurier illustration, in *Punch* for March 22, 1862; and there were David Bates's morbid verses waiting to be parodied as the Duchess's Lullaby,

'Speak gently to the little child,
Its love be sure to gain;
Teach it in accents soft and mild,
It may not long remain.'

The elongation of the Trial of the Knave of Hearts from one page to two chapters may have been suggested to Dodgson by his visit to the Assize Court on July 13, 1863, of which he notes that he heard 'some very petty cases, but they were interesting to me, as I have seen so little of trials'. To increase the 'Evidence', the nonsense verses 'She's All My Fancy Painted Him', were resuscitated from *The Comic Times* and revised to fit.

That same July Dodgson was having trial pages of *Alice's Adventures* set up by the Oxford University Press, and was still hoping to illustrate the book himself, even going so far as to prepare a block on wood—a half-length of Alice—which Thomas Woolner the Pre-Raphaelite looked at and 'condemned the arms, which he says I *must* draw from the life'.

He was meeting and photographing several artists such as Rossetti and Arthur Hughes that autumn, besides the editor and playwriter Tom Taylor, and they are likely to have dissuaded him from continuing with his own attempts as an illustrator. Reverting to Duckworth's suggestion of asking Tenniel to illustrate *Alice*, Dodgson got an introduction from Tom Taylor and called on him on January 25, 1864. Tenniel was interested, asked to see the complete story, and wrote on April 5 to tell Dodgson that he was willing to undertake the task.

As Dodgson could not illustrate his stories himself, he did the next best thing, he employed an expert artist to make the illustrations which he could see in his own mind but lacked the skill to reproduce on paper, paying for the work himself and, so far as possible, 'using' the artist as if he were a piece of machinery hired for the purpose. This explains why Tenniel's illustrations are so much a part of the two *Alice* books that no other artist has ever come near to equalling them; the same is also true of *Sylvie and Bruno*, though to a lesser extent, the book being less clearly imagined by the author, and Harry Furniss falling short of Tenniel's skill as an artist. It also explains Tenniel's repugnance to illustrate *Through the Looking-Glass* and his warning to Furniss, 'Lewis Carroll is impossible . . . I'll give you a week, old chap; *you* will never put up with that fellow a day longer.'

Not only did Dodgson pay for the illustrations to his books, but he paid also to have them printed, merely employing Messrs Macmillan & Co to publish them on a commission basis. The work was done by the Clarendon Press at Oxford; the complete book in galley-proofs was sent to Macmillans on December 16, 1864; Tenniel checked his last proofs by the middle of June; the Press printed off 2,000 copies and forty-eight were bound up early in July, most if not all of which Dodgson sent out as presents to his friends young and old, Alice receiving the first copy on July 4, 1865—three years to the day after the original picnic.

Before the book was properly out, however, Tenniel wrote that he was 'entirely dissatisfied with the printing of the pictures', and Dodgson—always scrupulously careful to give only of the best—withdrew it from circulation. He sent a letter to all who had received copies asking that they should be returned, and he retrieved in this way thirty-four copies which he gave to children's hospitals where all but two speedily disintegrated. The sixteen copies which chanced to survive from this first four dozen, which constituted the First Issue of the First Edition of *Alice's Adventures in*

Wonderland are now among the most valuable books of the last hundred years, specimens having been known to fetch as much as £5,000 each. The remaining 1,952 were sold (in unbound sheets) to Messrs Appleton of New York who issued 1,000 with a new title-page (dated 1866)—thus making the Second Issue of the First Edition. These title-pages were printed at Oxford and supplied with the sheets. Title-pages for the remaining 952 copies were subsequently printed in America—thus making the Third Issue of the First Edition. It was also 'pirated' in the U.S.A. in serial form, appearing in the December 1866 and January 1867 numbers of *Merryman's Monthly*.

Meanwhile Dodgson had the book reprinted by Messrs Clay of London, and it was published by Macmillans early in December 1865, though it was dated 1866; Dodgson received the first copy on November 9, and Tenniel gave his 'approval' later in the month.

This was the Second Edition, of which 2,000 copies were printed, and Dodgson calculated that if all copies were sold, he would still be £200 out of pocket, 'But if a second 2,000 could be sold it would cost £300, and bring in £500, thus squaring accounts and any further sale would be a gain, but that I can hardly hope for.'

By the time of his death some 180,000 copies had been sold, which suggests that he made some £18,000 out of this book alone—the equivalent of £100,000 in today's purchasing values, and that, moreover, at a time when there was virtually no income tax.

Alice's Adventures did not achieve immediate fame, nor even great sales according to the modest figures of a century ago. It did not go 'out of print' (i.e. when the first 4,000 copies were disposed of, and Dodgson's loss over the first edition was balanced by sales) until October 1866, the first copies of the '5th thousand' reaching him on December 1. And the early reviewers had not treated it as anything out of the ordinary; *The Athenaeum* commented that 'Mr Carroll has laboured hard . . . and we acknowledge the hard labour . . . a stiff, overwrought story', and *The Illustrated Times* thought it 'too extravagantly absurd to produce more diversion than disappointment and irritation'. But the *Pall Mall Gazette* gave it first place among the season's children's books, which included works by Jean Ingelow, William Gilbert, Ballantyne and Manville Fenn, 'This delightful little book is a children's feast and triumph of nonsense . . . never inhuman, never inelegant, never tedious'; 'a glorious artistic treasure' wrote *The Reader*'s reviewer: 'a book to put on one's shelf as an antidote to a fit of the blues'.

But it speedily began to creep into literature. Thirty years after its publication Charlotte in *The Golden Age* can tell the story of Alice's adventures to her dolls as if it had been 'Cinderella' or 'Puss in Boots', the author assuming naturally that every reader knew the book intimately.

As early as August 1866 Dodgson thought of writing a sequel to *Alice's Adventures* which would use up what he remembered of several more stories told to the three Liddell girls. But considering the illustrations so very important a part of the book, he decided not to begin writing it until he had his artist waiting to illustrate it. The trouble was that Tenniel refused to do it; one book by Lewis Carroll was all he felt, in 1866, that he could stand. So Dodgson made pilgrimage round the artists of the day, beginning with 'Dicky' Doyle who had illustrated *The King of the Golden River* for Ruskin. W. S. Gilbert, then known more for his illustrations to his father's children's stories and his own *Bab Ballads* was tried; and then Sir Noel Paton whose paintings of fairies he admired so much. Paton was too ill to undertake it, and insisted that 'Tenniel is *the* man'; and in June 1868 Tenniel consented to illustrate the projected book 'at such spare times as he can find'.

By August of that year Dodgson was busy writing *Looking-glass House*, and a chance meeting while staying with his uncle Skeffington Lutwidge in Onslow Square solved the question of what Alice should find the greatest difference after passing through the Looking-glass. A little cousin called Alice Raikes was playing in the garden, and Dodgson called her in. 'Would you like to come and see something which is rather puzzling?' he asked, and led her to a tall mirror across the corner of the room.

'"Now," he said, giving me an orange, "first tell me which hand you have got that in." "The right," I said. "Now," he said, "go and stand before that glass, and tell me which hand the little girl you see there has got it in." After some perplexed contemplation, I said, "The left hand." "Exactly," he said, "and how do you explain that?" I couldn't explain it, but seeing that some solution was expected, I ventured, "If I was on the *other* side of the glass, wouldn't the orange still be in my right hand?" I can remember his laugh. "Well done, little Alice," he said. "The best answer I've had yet."

'I heard no more then, but in after years was told that he said that had given him his first idea for *Through the Looking-Glass* . . .'

Not the first idea, of course, but the final twist. For the story originated, as Alice Liddell recorded, in several told to her long before the *Wonderland* picnic, 'particularly the ones to do with chessmen, which are dated by the period when we were excitedly learning chess'. The *Diaries* for that period are lost, but we may perhaps assume that the year was 1859, since in *Through the Looking-Glass* Alice tells Humpty-Dumpty that her age is 'seven years and six months'; as she was born on May 4 (the date of the Mad Tea Party) 1852, this gives November 4 (compare the boys making the bonfire in Chapter 1) 1859.

Dodgson's diary being missing, we cannot check what actually happened that day, but the meeting with the Red Queen in the 'Garden of Live Flowers' and the adventure of the train may date from the occasion when he visited the three children on holiday in April 1863. This was at Charlton Kings, near Cheltenham, where they were staying with Dean Liddell's mother who lived at 'Hetton Lawn'. On April 4 Dodgson records:

'Reached Cheltenham by 11.30 a.m. I found Alice waiting with Miss Prickett at the station, and walked with them to Charlton Kings, about one and a half miles. In the afternoon, we went a large party in the carriage up to Birdlip, where Ina, Alice and Miss Prickett got out, and walked back with me over Leckhampton Hill. Except for the high wind, the day could hardly have been better for the view; the children were in the wildest spirits.'

Doubtless those wild spirits demanded a story, and Miss Prickett, or 'Pricks', was the model for the Red Queen— 'one of the thorny kind' as the earlier editions of the book had it—whom Dodgson later described as 'the concentrated essence of all governesses'.

Miss Prickett may well have urged her charges to go 'Faster! Faster!' and may even have produced dry biscuits to refresh them—and once again the important business of education as imparted by her was there to form the basis for many conversations in the story.

Dodgson spent most of the next day with the Liddells at Hetton Lawn, and though he left Charlton Kings next day, he rejoined them a week later on their train journey home. 'We had a very merry journey to Oxford together', he records—and with such a raconteur as a companion they may well have expected the train to jump over a brook at any moment!

When he came to write *Through the Looking-Glass* Dodgson was making a more conscious literary effort than in writing out the Adventures Underground for Alice; and he had also time to let his various recollected stories simmer down. His method of writing seems to have been to collect scraps which 'came' to him and recollections of stories which he had told, besides suggestions growing out of books, pictures, and even topical events which would have meaning for Alice and her sisters while seeming mere fancy to the ordinary reader.

For a topical example Henry Luke Paget, later Bishop of Chester, who was an undergraduate at Christ Church about 1870, used to recall that, 'Alice, for instance, can buy two eggs cheaper than one at the Sheep's shop. "Only you must eat them both", said the Sheep, and a Christ Church undergraduate knew that if he ordered one boiled egg he was served with two, but one was invariably bad.'

Perhaps another idea, that for the Anglo-Saxon Messengers with their appropriate 'attitudes', came from a performance at the Christ Church theatricals on December 5, 1863 of Robert Brough's burlesque *Alfred the Great* in which a particular point was made of the Anglo-Saxon setting; both Dodgson and the Liddell children were in the audience.

Far more important than this, however, was the 'Stanza of Anglo-Saxon Poetry' that Dodgson had written at Croft at the end of 1855, which ran,

> ' 'Twas bryllyg, and the slythy toves
> Did gyre and gymble in the wabe;
> All mimsy were the borogoves;
> And the mome raths outgrabe.'

In this version, which is preserved in *Mischmasch* and was first published by Collingwood in *The Lewis Carroll Picture Book* in 1899, the stanza is followed by learned notes parodying those in an actual text, giving the meanings of the strange words. This was obviously impossible to transfer as it stood to *Through the Looking Glass*, but the meanings must be given somehow; Dodgson accordingly introduced Humpty-Dumpty with his appropriate Nursery Rhyme and developed him into the kind of burlesque professor who could properly give Alice a lecture on etymology. This also gave the opportunity for the introduction of the theory of 'portmanteau' words—which does not occur in the notes to the 1855 'Stanza of Anglo-Saxon Poetry'. In fact the real portmanteau words occur in the rest of the 'Jabberwocky' poem which was written at a different time (the date, unfortunately, is not preserved) while Dodgson was 'staying with his cousins, the Misses Wilcox, at Whitburn, near Sunderland. To while away an evening the whole party sat down to a game of verse-making, and "Jabberwocky" was his contribution.'

The party probably included a mutual cousin of Dodgson and the Wilcoxes, the poetess Menella Bute Smedley, and the substance of the poem parodies her much longer versification of a German legend, 'The Shepherd of the Giant Mountains', which first appeared in *Sharpe's London Magazine* in March 1846, with a Griffin in place of the Jabberwock nesting in an incredibly 'Gothick' oak tree beneath whose shade, in lieu of the Tumtum tree, a 'beamish boy' the Shepherd Gottschalk waited to slay it with a weapon that might well have been described as 'vorpal'.

'Jabberwocky' was not the only poem of an earlier date which Dodgson adapted for the new book and invented a character to suit. In *The Train* for October 1856 appeared his parody of Wordsworth's 'Resolution and Independence, or The Leechgatherer' called 'Upon the Lonely Moor', which he improved into the ballad 'A-sitting on a Gate' (to be sung to the tune of Thomas Moore's 'I give thee all, I can no more, tho' poor the off'ring be') and invented the character of the White Knight (as he admitted in 1893) 'to suit the speaker in the poem'.

Other ideas in the book may have originated in verses and pictures in *Punch*, of which Dodgson was an earnest student, and some of the ideas may have been shared with the Liddells and woven into stories during the previous ten years.

'Allow me to disagree with you,' says the Plum Pudding getting up in the dish and bowing to the diner who is about to help himself in the drawing by Edward Bradley ('Cuthbert Bede', author of *Mr Verdant Green*) on January 19, 1861; Tenniel's cartoon 'Law and Lunacy: Or, A Glorious Oyster Season for the Lawyers' (January 25, 1862) revives the saying: 'No more sense than an oyster' in a feast that suggests the orgy of the Walrus and the Carpenter. 'Ballad from Bedlam' contains such useful hints as:

'The elephant with cheerful voice
Sings blithely on the spray,'

while Looking-Glass Insects may have been an improvement on George du Maurier's collections of 'Specimens not yet included in the Collection at Regents Park' in June and August 1869 which include 'The Umbrella Bird', 'The Scissor-Wing Brush-Tail Razor-Bill' and the 'Tromboniferous Windbird'—which have to be seen to be believed.

Literature also played its part, usually subconsciously if the White Queen owes anything to Mrs Wragg in Wilkie

Collins's *No Name* or the White Knight to Hudibras—or the opening passages about Alice, Dinah and the kittens to a parody of Dickens's *Cricket on the Hearth* in *Blackwood's Magazine*, November 1845 (as Kathleen Tillotson suggests in the Autumn 1950 number of *English*); far more obviously in 'The Garden of Live Flowers' which follows Section XXII of Tennyson's *Maud*, particularly the stanza,

> 'There had fallen a splendid tear
>   From the passion-flower at the gate.
> She is coming, my dove, my dear;
>   She is coming, my life, my fate.
> The red rose cries, "She is near, she is near";
>   And the white rose weeps, "She is late";
> The larkspur listens, "I hear, I hear";
>   And the lily whispers "I wait".'

The passion-flower gave way to the tiger-lily when the religious origin of its name was pointed out to Dodgson, but otherwise all the flowers may be found in the poem. But the Garden may have been invented on a late visit to the Liddells, whose younger sisters were Rhoda ('Rose') born 1860; and Violet, born 1864—of whom the Tiger-lily might well say: 'You keep your head under the leaves, and snore away there, till you know no more what's going on in the world, than if you were a bud.'

It must not be thought that either of the *Alice* books is derivative; they are both original with the absolute originality of sheer genius. All the various 'originals' and suggestions served as so many sparks to touch off the sleeping gunpowder of Dodgson's imagination.

'*Alice* and the *Looking-Glass* are made up almost wholly of bits and scraps, single ideas which came of themselves', wrote Dodgson in April 1887 after the two books had been made into an operetta by Henry Savile Clarke. 'In writing it [*Alice's Adventures Underground*] out, I added many fresh ideas, which seemed to grow of themselves upon the original stock; and many more were added when, years afterwards, I wrote it all over again for publication; but (this may interest some readers of *Alice* to know) every such idea and nearly every word of the dialogue, *came of itself*. Sometimes an idea comes at night, when I have had to get up and strike a light to note it down—sometimes when out on a lonely winter walk, when I have had to stop, and with half-frozen fingers jot down a few words which should keep the new-born idea from perishing—but whenever or however it comes, *it comes of itself*. I cannot set invention going like a clock, by any voluntary winding up; nor do I believe that any *original* writing (and what other writing is worth preserving?) was ever so produced. . . .'

And, in reference to *The Hunting of the Snark*, but the answer is equally applicable to *Alice* (by which I designate the two books *Alice's Adventures in Wonderland* and *Through the Looking-Glass, and What Alice Found There*), Dodgson wrote in the same article,

'Periodically I have received courteous letters from strangers begging to know whether [it] is an allegory, or contains some hidden moral, or is a political satire; and for all such questions I have but one answer, "*I don't know!*" . . .'

Furthermore, he wrote in a letter towards the end of his life, also about the *Snark*:

'"I'm very much afraid I didn't mean anything but nonsense! Still, you know, words mean more than we mean to express when we use them; so a whole book ought to mean a great deal more than the writer meant." '

But consciously—and for several skins at least of that

fascinating onion the Subconscious—Dodgson told stories to children, following whatever development came into his logical mind, whatever new twist was given by some sudden question or misunderstanding from his audience, or whatever path a conscious or unconscious literary, dramatic or visual recollection might lead him—transmuted by the act of creation.

'One thing that made his stories particularly charming to a child,' wrote Gertrude Chataway, to whom *The Hunting of the Snark* (1876) was dedicated, 'was that he often took his cue from her remarks—a question would set him off on quite a new trail of ideas, so that one felt one had somehow helped to make the story, and it seemed a personal possession. It was the most lovely nonsense conceivable, and I naturally revelled in it. His vivid imagination would fly from one subject to another, and was never tied down in any way by the probabilities of life.'

Those who have told impromptu stories to children know how easy and natural it is to weave such fantasies as Dodgson wove, and by what means they are born and grow and suffer sudden and unexpected changes and developments; only our stories are but clay models, and into his the genius of Lewis Carroll breathed the breath of life.

Also we, like all subsequent writers, are under his influence. Lewis Carroll has so permeated our thoughts—subconsciously and unknowingly far more than consciously—that we can seldom do more than imitate. *Alice* is so much a part of the cultural heritage of the western world that it is hard to realise its uniqueness or to see how startlingly new it was.

About *Alice* Dodgson wrote: 'I can guarantee that the books have no religious teaching whatever in them—in fact they do not teach anything at all.'

To see how utterly different this was from all that had gone before, one has but to read *The Water Babies* (1863), an absolute orgy of self-conscious didacticism in which the fancy moves awkwardly, even guiltily, and the moral purpose is underlined throughout.

Although Catherine Sinclair in *Holiday House* had raised her voice as early as 1839 against the children's books of the period which, in their eagerness to instruct, had outlawed humour and imagination from the nursery, she had not been able to do much herself. Harry and Laura were more like real children than Maria Edgeworth's Rosamund or Matilda could ever be, and a moment's natural naughtiness was not underlined as the first step to hell as it would have been by Mr Barlow in Mrs Sherwood's sin-obsessed *Fairchild Family*. Uncle David could also tell a 'Wonderful Story' in which a fairy-tale giant wandered through mazes of delightful nonsense; but even there a definite moral emerged.

But in the forties and fifties the barriers were being broken down just a little; fairy tales were allowed into the more broadminded nurseries; Thackeray flouted convention with *The Rose and the Ring* (1855), though even he was forced to excuse himself in the unsuitable subtitle 'A Fireside Pantomime', and the nursery-rhyme collections had been reinforced by the quiet appearance of Edward Lear's *Book of Nonsense* in 1846 where the 'limericks' (though not then so called) were modelled on the booklets in the same verse-form which he had known as a child about 1822.

Nevertheless these earlier premonitions of the dawn of levity were always at one remove from the child. Either they were set in a fairy world, a world of the past, or else they were kept at a suitable distance by the footlights of verse—as even W. B. Rands does in *Lilliput Levee* which appeared a year before *Alice's Adventures in Wonderland*. Rands knew something of the wonderland of a child's imagination, but seems not to have had the courage to take it seriously, so that his moments of freedom become a positive burlesque of wishful thinking.

The revolutionary nature of 'Lewis Carroll's' achievement cannot be exaggerated. Alice was a genuine child who, instead of tripping her demure way round the parish with the Mays in *The Daisy Chain* or emulating Mary Charlesworth's *Ministering Children*, danced joyously into Wonderland, turning all Miss Prickett's teachings topsy-turvy, joking with the Duchess about the necessity for there being a moral in every story, and came home to her Victorian nursery without a spot on her character—or a suspicion of having learnt anything more serious than the rules of a Caucus Race or the way to cut Looking-Glass cake.

'The directness of such a work was a revolution in its sphere,' wrote Harvey Darton in his *Children's Books in England* in 1932. 'It was the coming to the surface, powerfully and permanently, the first unapologetic, undocumented appearance in print, for readers who sorely needed it, of liberty of thought in children's books. Henceforth fear had gone, and with it shy disquiet. There was to be in hours of pleasure no more dread about the moral value, the ponderable, measured quality and extent, of the pleasure itself. It was to be enjoyed and even promoted with neither forethought nor remorse.'

Harvey Darton further maintains that while '*The Water Babies* is a very fine period piece, almost, indeed, a museum piece, the *Alices* will never be put in a museum, because they will neither die nor grow out of fashion.' During the thirty-five years since he wrote this, *Alice* has moved up in the literary scale and been accepted officially as a classic for the adult—for without question the reader of mature age gets much out of it that is lost upon the child, or perceived in a different way. It is partly as an excuse for this new attitude that critics have tried so hard to prove that Dodgson meant very much more by his two stories than mere light-hearted amusement for children.

With those who believe that an extremely careful and detailed religious, political or mathematical allegory is intended, it seems hardly necessary to deal. Except in an odd momentary flash such double meanings are not the work of the subconscious mind—and Dodgson's conscious intentions seem hardly open to doubt. The subconscious as explored by the psycho-analysts such as Professor Empson or Dr Greenacre may yield a few clues as to Dodgson's character and suggest a few possible twists or preoccupations which could have produced certain incidents in *Alice*; but they *were* subconscious and have no direct bearing on the stories. If, however, the adult reader sees them as composed of Freudian symbols, there may be some reluctance in giving them to a child to read; the modern preoccupation with the new and only half-understood science of psychology some-times tends to see *Alice* as full of horrors, from Alice's fear of going out like a candle to the Queen's decapitation complex.

It seems unlikely that more than one child in a million will see anything but amusement in *Alice*—and it is im-possible to predict the odd child, who might equally have been frightened by the most unexpected thing elsewhere. Tenniel's drawing of Alice with the long neck has been found frightening, and Dodgson himself hesitated over the possible terrors of the Jabberwock. But it might be the White King's threat to Haigha; 'If you do that again, I'll have you buttered'—which to one child was the funniest line in either book; just as (to take an actual case) a mother discussing what books frightened children confessed that *Peter Pan* was the terror of her childhood—not because of any of the doings of Captain Hook, but because Mr Darling lived for a while in the dog kennel!

Setting aside this possibility, it seems only fair to point out that decapitation, change of size, the Dormouse in the teapot,* or the Red Knight falling into his own helmet are quite unreal to children, and a part of their natural imagination which can invent for itself, and acclaim as riotously funny 'horrific' ideas which far outdo the experiences of Red Riding Hood's grandmother or the Myth of Cronos.

That a number of modern children find little enjoyment in *Alice* is not a sign of a more fastidious and humanitarian mind, but of lesser powers of imagination. The modern accent is once again upon the inculcation of facts, as it was in the days before Catherine Sinclair registered the first effective protest against 'the reading which might be a relaxation from study becoming a study in itself'. The willing suspension of disbelief becomes harder to achieve, and the attempt to do so has become far less common or necessary since there are so many more books—and other occupations—from which today's children may choose.

Alice, moreover, was at its most popular among children when reading aloud was still customary. The ideal age is from four till eight, and often by the time it can be read easily the perfect moment is passed, for—to generalise—the only decade in life during which *Alice* does not appeal is from eight to eighteen. Sophistication has lowered the age-limit which would probably have been at twelve in Dodgson's day; the appeal to the 'eighteen-plus' group is by no

---

* Victorian children actually kept their pet dormice in nests made for them in old tea-pots during their periods of hibernation.

means new—*Alice* was the rage among undergraduates by the mid seventies, and the language of 'Jabberwocky' became current in public schools at much the same time.

A census carried out by *The Academy* (July 2, 1898) found *Alice* at the top of the list of the ten children's books most in demand, the other nine being, in descending order, *Robinson Crusoe*, Lang's *Fairy Books*, Hans Andersen, *The Water Babies*, Mrs Molesworth's stories, *Eric, or Little by Little*, *The Jungle Books*, Grimm, and *Treasure Island*. Doubtless fond uncles may have raised the percentage for Farrar and Kingsley, but the list squares well with other contemporary evidence.

The immediate literary effect of *Alice's Adventures in Wonderland* was to let loose the imprisoned waters of levity —which became a positive flood when *Through the Looking-Glass* appeared at the end of 1871.

'*Alice* is always being imitated,' complained Andrew Lang in 1895, and Harvey Darton as late as 1932 noted that: 'The fault of the many imitators of Lewis Carroll—who are to this day a permanent plague to all editors and publishers of literature for children—is that they force the transition from one nature to the other; they invent, but they have not the logic.'

It was Dodgson's logic which gave the particular turn to his humour and supplied him with the tools wherewith to construct his masterpiece; it was his training in formal logic, as Peter Alexander, himself a professional logician, points out, which enabled him to build 'a setting within which inconsistency would appear inevitable, and so convincing; or, more precisely, showed him how to *use* a common fairy tale setting to contain more than any normal fairy tale ever contained.' The purely logical sequence of reasoning from an illogical premise—usually a phrase in popular use but used loosely—is well exemplified by the conversation between Alice and the Cheshire Cat on 'getting somewhere', or by the discussion with the White King on the hay diet.

' "There's nothing like eating hay when you are faint," he remarked to her as he munched away.

"I should think throwing cold water over you would be better," Alice suggested—"or some sal-volatile."

"I didn't say there was nothing *better*," the King replied, "I said there was nothing *like* it." '

Professor Alexander further points out how wrong Alexander Woollcott was in talking of a discrepancy between 'the man who wrote the most enchanting nonsense in the English language', and the 'puttering, fussy, fastidious, didactic old bachelor', and comments:

'For the will to escape was joined with the ability to escape; an ability which depended on a detailed knowledge of, and interest in, logic. Without Dodgson the pedantic logician, Carroll the artist would have been of considerably less importance; there was no discrepancy.'

Dodgson was a consistent figure throughout his life; his habits and idiosyncrasies were all there before *Through the Looking-Glass* was published, they merely grew more pronounced and less accommodating in his later years.

The basis for the methodical exactness of detail which his contemporaries at Christ Church found so irritating was his scrupulous sense of duty: 'Oh that I might hear "Well done, good and faithful servant",' was an early prayer committed to his diary, but it was a prayer which grew more and more urgent as the allotted span of his earthly life drew towards its end. From this sprang his hypersensitive care over the preparation of his books; his care to give the best he could gave the finish and precision of *Alice*, but also the direct preaching which mars *Sylvie and Bruno* from the literary point of view. This care was known only to himself, but his scrupulous endeavour to give the most perfect result possible on the mechanical side is shown by his withdrawal of the first edition of *Alice's Adventures in Wonderland* because the printing was not up to the highest standard, by his attempt to recall the sixtieth thousand of *Through the Looking-Glass* for the same reason, and by his refusal to publish the first printing of *The Nursery Alice* because the colours were too gaudy. Fearing that copies of a book might be printed too hurriedly to meet a sudden demand, he wrote to his publishers,

'As to how many copies we can sell I care absolutely nothing; the one only thing I *do* care for is, that all copies that *are* sold shall be artistically first-rate.'

This thoroughly praiseworthy attitude only became excessive when Dodgson began trying to make everyone else as scrupulously honest as himself, running the Senior Common Room at Christ Church, of which he was Curator for almost ten years, on these lines, and writing notes to the Post Master about the dishonesty of having the mail collected a few minutes earlier than the time advertised on the letter boxes, and to the chaplain for reciting the Creed too fast.

His life was ordered with great strictness and method. Early rising, scripture reading before attendance at Chapel (Oxford Cathedral in the case of Christ Church), lunch of a few biscuits and a glass of sherry so as not to interrupt his work; long walks several times a week for the good of his health; dinner in Hall, but only a short time in the Senior Common Room thereafter; a post-prandial snooze firmly negatived, and work again until late at night. Then, when increasing insomnia left the mind apt to wander over trivial or harmful matters, the rigid discipline of Pillow Problems—mathematical and geometrical puzzles that could be worked out on the blackboard of the mind.

The scrupulous care for every detail made letter-writing a major occupation, and Dodgson kept a register from 1861 until a few days before his death which ran to over 98,000 entries with notes and cross-references as described in his pamphlet *Eight or Nine Wise Words About Letter-Writing* (1890).

When going away he worked out exactly what he would need (just as, before beginning a letter he chose exactly the right sized sheet of paper to fill completely), wrapped each article carefully in paper before packing any of them, and sent his luggage in advance (nearly as many trunks as the Baker, one might think!), carrying a small black bag himself. He was also careful to take, in a specially made purse, all the exact sums of money he would need on the journey, each in a separate division ready for use.

In the black bag would be a number of toys and puzzles to produce if he were lucky enough to share a compartment with children, and many child-friendships began in this way. Many more began at the seaside, Dodgson spending a couple of months at Eastbourne each summer after his father's death in 1868, after which his sisters set up house together at 'The Chestnuts', Guildford—where also he was a frequent visitor.

Little girls met on the shore would be told stories or presented with safety-pins before paddling, but there was always the scrupulous application to the parent or guardians before the friendship was well under way. Later in life Dodgson had child visitors—often of the stage-children whom he met after *Alice* was dramatised in 1886—who would stay under the care of his landlady at Eastbourne, or with friends at Oxford.

Dodgson's sentimental relationship with his numerous child-friends has been the subject of some curiosity, not always of a charitable nature. It must be stressed again that the glorious escape from the stammer while in their society was a very strong incentive for Dodgson to seek these friendships; he was simply and honestly happy in the company of children, more so with girls—though earlier in his life there were many small boys among his friends, such as Greville MacDonald, Hallam Tennyson and Harry Liddell —who were more interested in his tales and puzzles, more orderly and less rampageous, and far better subjects for photography. Dodgson was an artist who never learnt to draw, though some charming sketches of children on the beach survive; he had the artist's genuine delight in beauty of form, and without it would not have been the finest photographer of children in the nineteenth century. After having exhausted the possibilities of grouping and costume, it is natural that he should have turned to nude models— always after careful consultation with the parents, and with scrupulous consideration for the child. In 1880, however, some ill-natured gossip must have got about, and Dodgson may suddenly have felt that his interest in nude photography contained the hidden seeds of sin. With his scrupulous honesty and devout sense of duty, he at once gave up photography altogether. But some years later he occasionally drew from the model in the studio of his friend Mrs Shute, widow of a Christ Church don, and he wrote to Harry Furniss who was illustrating *Sylvie and Bruno*, 'I wish I could dispense with all costume, naked children are so pure and lovely, but "Mrs Grundy" would be furious, it would never do. . . . You must remember that the work has to be seen, not only by children, but by their *Mothers*; and some *Mothers* are *awfully* particular. . . .'

The last photographs were taken in July 1880, a few months after another source of suspicion to 'awfully particular' mothers. Dodgson kissed one of his Oxford child-friends whom he thought was well under fourteen, only to discover that she was, in fact, seventeen; he was much upset and consulted his friend Canon Kitchin, who suggested interviewing the girl's father, another don, after which that storm in a teacup blew over.

The kissing of children in that sentimental age was much practised, and has not gone out completely even now. On the whole boys were apt to object early to wholesale and promiscuous osculations, while girls accepted them as natural, up to the dividing line, 'where the stream and river meet', which was set at fourteen. Dodgson was merely being an adult of his period in bestowing frequent kisses on his child-friends—and he could make capital game of excessive kissing as is shown in a delightful letter to the child-actress Isa Bowman who had begged for 'Millions of hugs and kisses'.

'Millions must mean 2 millions at least . . . and I don't think you'll manage it more than 20 times a minute—[a sum follows]. I couldn't go on hugging and kissing more than 12 hours a day; and I wouldn't like to spend *Sundays* that way. So you see it would take 23 *weeks* of hard work. Really, my dear child, *I cannot spare the time*.'

It has been suggested that Dodgson fell in love with Alice Liddell, possibly even while she was a child, and was 'sent about his business' by Mrs Liddell, whose ambition to marry all her daughters into the titled aristocracy was a standing joke at Christ Church. This is a wildly unlikely suggestion; the Christ Church undergraduates thought that Dodgson had proposed for Lorina and been rejected—but they had also thought that his interest in the children was a 'cover' for a flirtation with Miss Prickett the governess. Dodgson was unusual to the extent that a grown man's interest in children had to be explained by the average undergraduate in some such way.

Mrs Liddell may well have felt jealous of Dodgson's influence over her children; he considered her quite right in forbidding Lorina to visit him unchaperoned after the age of thirteen. But she disliked Dodgson for other reasons. One of her protégés was a titled undergraduate, Lord Newry; she wished the rules to be stretched a point to allow him to give a dance, but Dodgson the scrupulous would not allow a golden tassel to sway his fairness of judgment, and he vetoed this when it was brought up at the college meeting. 'I have been out of her good graces ever since Lord Newry's business', wrote Dodgson in his diary on October 28, 1862, and Mrs Liddell's coldness, though lifted a little, closed down even more firmly as time went on. For Dodgson found himself compelled to attack Dean Liddell's administration of college affairs more and more, beginning with an acrimonious correspondence in January 1864 over the appointment of Junior Students, and going on to the public ridicule of the architectural alterations at Christ Church satirised in *The New Belfry* (1872), *The Vision of the Three T's* (1873) and other of the *Notes by an Oxford Chiel*. Finally his letters to the *Pall Mall Gazette* in November 1874, which prevented Liddell's extravagant scheme for building cloisters round Tom Quad, completed the rift.

But long before this Alice had become only a memory; 'Alice seems changed a good deal, and hardly for the better—probably going through the usual awkward state of transition', he noted on May 11, 1865, when she was just thirteen, and this seems to have been almost their last meeting. Even by then the dream-flowers of Wonderland were 'Pluck'd in a far-off land'—and Alice soon became a dream-child herself to whom Dodgson looked back with special gratitude for 'the happy summer days' and for the spark which she had struck from his genius which had resulted in *Wonderland* and *Through the Looking-Glass*.

Doubtless a natural pang of jealousy came Dodgson's way now and then as one or another of his favourite child-friends took to herself a husband. Isa Bowman, one of the half-dozen or so who came nearest to usurping Alice's place, remembered how furious he was when she came to announce her engagement, and how he tried to cover it up by snatching the posy from her belt and flinging it out of the window, exclaiming 'You know how I hate flowers!'

But this was the pang of a moment, and he could write wisely and charmingly to an ex-child-friend on her marriage and continue the friendship to her children. During the last ten years of his life he found older girls more congenial, and made several friends from the High School, and also from the newly founded women's colleges. Several of his own nieces were educated in Oxford, and they found him as charming and attentive an uncle as any of his child-friends could have done.

IV. After Alice

None of Dodgson's favourites after Alice brought out the magic spark again. Although it is dedicated to Gertrude Chataway, *The Hunting of the Snark* owed nothing to her. It was the last of his works that came to him with unforced compulsion, and Dodgson narrated how its odd construction began on July 18, 1874 while taking exercise near Guildford.

'I was walking on a hillside alone, one bright summer day, when suddenly there came into my head one line of verse— one solitary line—"For the Snark *was* a Boojum, you see." I knew not what it meant, then; I know not what it means now; but I wrote it down; and, some time afterwards [on July 22], the rest of the stanza occurred to me, that being its last line; and so by degrees, at odd moments during the next year or two, the rest of the poem pieced itself together, that being its last stanza.'

By November he had written three out of the final eight 'fits' of the poem, and asked Henry Holiday to illustrate it as it 'would some day be introduced in a book he was contemplating; but as the latter would certainly not be ready for some considerable time, he thought of printing the poem for private circulation in the first instance'.

The poem grew and grew, however, and by the following November, when he considered it finished (though there were still only 88 out of the final 141 stanzas), Dodgson had decided to publish it separately and not wait to incorporate it in *Sylvie and Bruno* or even include it in the contemplated collection of his humorous verse which appeared as *Rhyme?*

And Reason? in 1883. He was still to add two more 'fits', the last stanza added being written on January 19, 1876, and the whole poem published on March 29.

The Hunting of the Snark was not received as whole-heartedly as the *Alices* had been.

'Much of the effect of *Alice* was got by the contrast of her childish niceness and naturalness with the absurd and evanescent character of the creatures in Wonderland', wrote Andrew Lang, reviewing it in *The Academy*. And he pointed out that this time the reader sees the characters 'in themselves, he does not see them in the eyes of the child, who, as in *Alice*, takes them as natural persons in a world not understood.'

Perhaps for this reason the *Snark* has never had so wide an appeal to children as it has to adults. But it is, nevertheless, the only great nonsense poem of any length ever written and is indeed only challenged by such pieces of Dodgson's own as 'Jabberwocky', 'The Walrus and the Carpenter', and 'A-sitting on a Gate'; even such masterpieces as Lear's 'The Owl and the Pussy Cat' and 'The Pobble Who has No Toes' cannot rank quite so high.

Dodgson had not succeeded so well in *Phantasmagoria*, the amusing but undistinguished poem about the tribulations of a young ghost which gave its name to a volume of his miscellaneous poems grave and gay, nearly all of which was published in 1869. After the *Snark*, the fountain of his genius seemed to dry up, and little else that he wrote would be remembered today, were it not for his earlier successes.

But far from ceasing to write, he laboured more and more unsparingly, though few of his later works were of a purely literary nature. *Euclid and his Modern Rivals* (1879) stands out, not merely as the only one of the mathematical works of 'Charles L. Dodgson, M.A., Senior Student and

Mathematical Lecturer of Christ Church, Oxford' which a non-mathematician can read with enjoyment or even understanding, but in Falconer Madan's words, 'One of the outstanding examples of serious argument cast in an amusing style.' The form is dramatic, and the 'improvers and simplifiers' of Euclid come in for reasoned ridicule, 'much fun results, with comic but conclusive discomfitures of all kinds'.

His most serious mathematical works of later years were a new edition of *Euclid I and II* in 1882, and the two volumes of problems, *Curiosa Mathematica*, 1888 and 1892. But he achieved another claim to fame in an unexpected sideline by the publication in 1884 (after several letters to *The St James's Gazette* on the subject) of *The Principles of Parliamentary Representation*, which Professor Duncan Black treats in his recent book on the subject as one of the most important works in the history of the theory and practice of voting.

Mathematics for children was attempted in 1885 with *A Tangled Tale*, a series of ten problems dressed up as stories which had appeared in Charlotte Yonge's magazine *The Monthly Packet* between 1880 and 1884. This contains delightful sparks of humour, besides the interest deriving from the clever problems, but seems rather a waste of his talents.

Dodgson had always been in the habit of inventing games for his child-friends; simple ones that were never written down like the picture-stories such as 'Mr C. and Mr T.' (preserved in the Appendix to the *Diaries* thanks to the memory of one of his child-friends), and the numerous riddles, to complicated games like Court Circular or Croquet Castles. Late in 1877 he invented 'Word-links' for Julia and Ethel Arnold, and developed it the next year as *Doublets*, under which title the rules were published as a small book in 1879 after the game had appeared in *Vanity Fair* and been played by its readers.

Doublets, which has been described as the father of cross-word puzzles, is the easiest of Dodgson's word-games, and the one which children still enjoy. The game is to turn one word into another of the same length by changing one letter at a time but always making a real word by each change. Thus to 'Drive PIG into STY' the chain runs 'WIG, WAG, WAY, SAY', scoring four points as against, for example, 'PEG, PEN, PAN, PAY, SAY', which would score five—the lowest score being the winner.

Two more word-games followed: *Misch-Masch* (1882) and *Syzygies* (1891), both clever but too complicated for any average child—or for many adults. A complex board-game, *Lanrick*, was invented in 1880, and the even more unusual *Circular Billiards for Two Players* (to be played on a round billiard table which he had specially constructed) ten years later. But meanwhile Dodgson's interest in logic had grown more and more to take the place of mathematics, and besides entering into learned controversies, personally or by way of periodical publications, with eminent logicians, he decided that children should be taught logic also.

His first, and most successful, attempt was his invention of *The Game of Logic* published as by Lewis Carroll in 1886, complete with miniature board and coloured counters. Dodgson described it in the Preface as an 'endless source of amusement', but when Marghanita Laski tried it on her children, as described in Derek Hudson's *Lewis Carroll*, she found that, though they began with enthusiasm, it proved too difficult after page thirteen!

Dodgson was not discouraged, however, and proceeded with logic for the young. In 1896 *Symbolic Logic: Part I.*

Elementary was published, and Part II was nearing completion (though never published) at the time of his death. Although this went into four editions in the year of publication, and has been highly praised by advanced students of logic, it too is far harder than its author realised. Dodgson used it with success at various girls' schools and among female undergraduates, but once again without Lewis Carroll to expound it, the charm is lost—though we can smile happily (if we do not have to solve them) over such Concrete Propositions as: '(1) Babies are illogical; (2) Nobody is despised who can manage a crocodile; (3) Illogical persons are despised. . . . *Answer*. Babies cannot manage crocodiles.'

As early as 1875 Dodgson was planning a volume to be called *Alice's Puzzle-Book*, which was to have a frontispiece by Tenniel, and it got so far as to be advertised as 'coming shortly' in his last book *Three Sunsets and Other Poems* (1898) under the title *Original Games and Puzzles*, illustrated by E. Gertrude Thomson.

Dodgson had made up riddles as early at least as 1855 when a verse example appeared in the family magazine *Mischmasch*,

> 'A monument—men all agree—
> Am I in all sincerity,
>   Half cat, half hindrance made.
> If head and tail removed should be,
> Then most of all you strengthen me;
> Replace my head, the stand you see
>   On which my tail is laid.'

More common still were the cleverly contrived acrostics in verse giving the names of the children to whom the various books were dedicated. Thus the lines at the end of *Through the Looking-Glass* give 'Alice Pleasance Liddell' by taking the first letters, the dedicatee of *The Nursery Alice* may be found by taking the second letter of each line, and of *Sylvie and Bruno Concluded* by taking the third, and there are many more. Several acrostic riddles are also preserved, some being included by Dodgson in *Rhyme? And Reason?*

The absorption with logic and puzzles did not prevent Dodgson from contemplating a further work of fiction. 'I should *much* like to write one more child's book before all writing power leaves me,' he wrote in 1876, and he already had ideas as to what it was to be. On June 24, 1867, he wrote in his diary two hours after midnight: 'I have spent some hours on a paper (I have had the idea for two or three days) for *Aunt Judy's Magazine*, to be called "Bruno's Revenge".' This very slight but rather pleasant fairy tale, with a discreet moral or parable (as befitted a contribution to the periodical edited by the author of *Parables from Nature*) appeared in the number for December 1867. The names of the two fairy children are obviously derived from Sylph and Brownie ('Broonie' in Scotland and the north of England) and admirably suit this little woodland tale.

Dodgson continued to make up stories about Sylvie and Bruno, two more being composed for Lord Salisbury's children when he was staying at Hatfield for the New Year of 1873 ('Bruno's Picnic' and probably 'Fairy Sylvie') and two years later he was telling the same children 'Prince Uggug', which harked back to the unpleasant boy Guggy of 'Crundle Castle' in *The Rectory Magazine*. Though often apt to agree with the robin in Mrs Hart's verses in *Aunt Judy's* for June 1867, 'But a great mistake it is, Boys were ever made at all!', Dodgson compensated for the detestable Uggug by the charming small-boyishness of Bruno, who indeed comes out better than the slightly over-sweet Sylvie.

Had he been content to make up a little volume of the

short tales about his fairy children, Dodgson might have produced a pleasant and lastingly entertaining book, even if it was definitely 'of its period' and a disappointment after the dateless quality of *Alice*. But he was not content so to do, and he continued for years to collect a mass of incidents, ideas and scraps of dialogue—'litterature' as he aptly described it—which he was determined to work up into an utterly new kind of book, as different as possible from his earlier successes. 'Anything which would have the effect of connecting the book with *Alice* would be absolutely disastrous. I am trying my very best to get out of the old groove,' he wrote to his illustrator Harry Furniss, though to begin with (when he engaged him in 1885) he had written: 'Now that you are found, I shall go back to my *Alice in Wonderland* style of work with every hope of making a success.'

Dodgson's new book, which appeared in two parts (each twice as long as *Wonderland*), *Sylvie and Bruno* (1889) and *Sylvie and Bruno Concluded* (1893), is an immensely clever work, a fairy tale, a nonsense story and a society novel fitted together with so much care, skill and cunning that one is tempted to attribute its failure to Prince Prigio's christening curse, 'My child, you shall be *too* clever!'

Certainly in *Sylvie and Bruno* Dodgson was taking his mission to teach far too seriously; he was determined to 'improve each shining hour', so that most of the 'novel' portion of the book becomes a tract on the Christian virtues which tends to make the characters exaggerated and unreal. The fairy children, however, pass through three stages doubling those intended in the construction: in 'Outland' they and all they meet are true Lewis Carroll creations strayed out of Wonderland into a nearby province; in 'Fairyland' they are still 'tricksy fays' but (as in 'Bruno's

Revenge') are tending towards over-sweetness and arti-
ficiality, and in the real world they appear (or make themselves felt) purely on the moral plain, almost as miniature
guardian angels.

Setting aside the 'real-life' portions of the book, Dodgson
was positively hampered by his determination to use
'Bruno's Revenge' and the other Hatfield stories. The fairies
in them were the whimsy fays over-refined by literary tradition—they are almost the fairies of 'flowers and fruits and
other winged things' against whom Andrew Lang was to
protest so bitterly in the Preface to the last of his Fairy
Books. Bruno, whether fairy or small human child, is given
'baby talk' which modern readers find hard to stomach.
There is scarcely a sign of it in the original 'Bruno's
Revenge', but by the eighties it had become an accepted,
even an expected convention. 'Dialect' was an extraordinary
disease which ran riot through later Victorian literature, the
greatest impetus coming from America with such popular
works as Leland's *Breitmann Ballads* and pidgin-English
poems supposed to be the work of a Chinaman, with *Uncle
Remus* and the 'slang' of Mark Twain's *Huckleberry Finn*;
and more indigenously with Kipling's *Barrack Room
Ballads* and F. Anstey's *Baboo Jabberjee*. In the literature of
childhood it reached the dimensions of an orgy in the
immensely popular *Helen's Babies* (1876). Even the greatest
writers about children felt constrained to use it to some
extent, as Mrs Molesworth showed in *Carrots* (1876) and
Herr Baby (1881), and it was only eradicated by the new
approach to childhood exemplified by Kenneth Grahame
and E. Nesbit.

Dodgson showed himself a typical man of his period by
using the accepted medium of speech for Bruno, and by
spreading the sentiment a little too thick whenever he got

the chance. He sat and gulped at *Little Lord Fauntleroy*, a great book perverted into a sentimental play for adults of easy emotions. He had a large number of contemporary children's books in his library at the time of his death, and perhaps could not always distinguish the good trends from the bad, though to counteract *Misunderstood* and Kipling's 'His Majesty the King' he had Mrs Ewing, Mrs Molesworth and George MacDonald.

Accepting the convention of baby-talk (though the story would be vastly improved by having a great deal less of it) the actual adventures of *Sylvie and Bruno* form a suitable and effective plot, with such characters as the Mad Gardener and the Professor every bit as worthy of immortality as the Mad Hatter or the White Knight. Edwin Dodgson tried to separate *The Story of Sylvie and Bruno* from the rest in 1904, but not very satisfactorily since his respect for his brother's memory forbade him to alter or add more than an odd word where absolutely necessary. But the plot, which might well be isolated and edited a little to good effect, runs somewhat as follows:

Sylvie and Bruno are the children of the Warden of Outland, a province of Fairyland, but far away from Elfland, which is the real heart of the Fairy world. The Warden has to visit Elfland where he hopes to be elected Emperor, and leaves his wicked brother and sister-in-law, Sibimet and Tabikat, to rule in Outland, advised by the Court Professor. These two conspire to make themselves King and Queen and to put their stupid and unpleasant son Uggug in Bruno's place as heir to the throne. They ill-treat the children so much that, with the help of the Professor and the Mad Gardener, they run away to look for their father, and find the road to Elfland by means of Sylvie's magic locket. On the way they pass through Dogland and have an amusing time with the canine population. Once in Elfland they become ordinary fairies, and live happily for a time, their daily life being described in such incidents as 'Bruno's Revenge' and 'Bruno's Picnic'. But at last the Professor arrives with the news that Sibimet and Tabikat are about to be crowned King and Queen, and he returns with Sylvie and Bruno to delay the coronation until the Warden can appear with his full powers as Emperor. When they reach Outland a great coronation banquet is about to begin, and to hold up the proceedings as much as possible the Professor prefaces it with his great Lecture which he has been preparing throughout the book. Half way through the banquet things begin to happen: Uggug turns into a porcupine, and the Warden arrives just in time to frustrate his brother's wicked plans. All ends happily with forgiveness and a beautiful sunset.

These adventures are punctuated with delicious incidents, inventions and remarks which might have come straight from Wonderland.

'"But what's the use of wearing umbrellas round one's knees?"

"In *ordinary* rain," the Professor admitted, "they would not be of much use. But if ever it rained horizontally, you know, they would be invaluable—simply invaluable!" '

Or again,

'The Professor put his hands over his ears with a look of dismay. "If you once let him begin a *Poem*," he said to Sylvie, "he'll never leave off again! He never does!"

"Did he ever begin a poem and not leave off again?" Sylvie enquired.

"Three times," said the Professor.'

Or the Professor's demonstration of Black Light,

'"What did you see in the box?" Sylvie enquired eagerly.
"I saw *nuffin*!" Bruno sadly replied. "It were too dark!"

"He has described the appearance of the thing exactly!"
the Professor exclaimed with enthusiasm. "Black Light,
and Nothing, look so extremely alike, at first sight, that I
don't wonder he failed to distinguish them!"...'

And finally the two best sets of verses, the Mad Gardener's
songs and 'Little Birds', of which (for the sake of variety) I
quote two stanzas which were *not* included in the book.
The first was altered to suit the context; the second omitted
so as not to overflow Harry Furniss's ingenious frameworks,

> 'He thought he saw a Cormorant
>   That nestled in a tree;
> He looked again, and found it was
>   A Double Rule of Three:
> "And all its mystery," he said,
>   "Is clear as day to me!"'

> 'Little Birds are seeking
>   Hecatombs of haws,
>   Dressed in snowy gauze:
> Dressed, I say, in fringes
> Half alive with hinges—
>   Thus they break the laws.'

Altogether *Sylvie and Bruno*, for all its shortcomings,
is a fascinating book, and is aptly described by Derek
Hudson as 'one of the most interesting failures in English
Literature'.

'Is all our life then but a dream?' asked Lewis Carroll in
the dedication to the first volume of this which he considered his greatest book. 'He had very good health and
was seldom out of sorts,' wrote a friend who knew him well;
but Dodgson worked the machine too hard, and the dis-

cipline which grew into the near-vice of asceticism, brought on insomnia, psychic migraine and a liability to acute bronchial infection. As early as 1883 he wrote to another friend 'I am not quite "the thing", and in fact am fit for little else than to lie on the sofa all day and read novels.' He complained in later life that he had little time for reading, but this meant serious works; he was, when 'on the sofa' an ardent novel reader, possessing and having read, often many times, the works of Dickens, Scott, the Brontës, Thackeray and his daughter, Mrs Craik, George Eliot, Meredith, Fenimore Cooper, both Kingsleys, MacDonald, Besant, Stevenson and Kipling, besides such current poets as Tennyson, Rossetti, Morris, Swinburne and Edwin Arnold —and probably many others; references to reading ceased in his later *Diaries*, and the Sale Catalogue of his library only mentions by name authors whose first editions happened to be sought after in 1898. He was certainly up to date, and still with a good individual taste, his favourite author at the time of his death being Kipling, and Barrie his favourite dramatist; the last play he saw was *The Little Minister*, 'a beautiful play, beautifully acted . . . a play I should like to see again and again'.

In 1891 he was writing to Harry Furniss that 'I have been rather seriously ill . . . I don't think I have any right to reckon much on the coming years, and there is a lot of work I want to finish before the end comes.'

But at Oxford there seemed to be no change in him, except that he became rather more aloof, almost a hermit some people thought. He refused invitations to dinner and, apart from longer and longer walks, spent most of his time in his rooms; he had given up his Lectureship in 1881, and ceased to be Curator of Common Room in 1892. But the tall, spare figure in clerical black, so upright that he seemed almost to be bending over backwards, with the rather delicate, wistful features and the iron-grey hair, worn full, turning towards white, was still a familiar figure in Tom Quad and in the roads round Oxford. Still, children would spot him in the distance as he strode round Merton Meadow or crossed the Parks, and rush to meet him with shouts of joy: 'It's Uncle Dodgson! Here comes Uncle Dodgson! Let's make a barrier across the path so that he can't pass!' While those less fortunate would at least return home full of excitement: 'I saw Mr Dodgson today!' He was still readily accessible, to children at least, in his big sitting-room at the corner of Tom Quad, while the index boxes and file-cabinets grew and multiplied round him—the room with the two turret closets off it overlooking St Aldates of which he once said to Isa Bowman: 'When you're grown up and married you must come and live here; then, when you and your husband quarrel, you can each live in a separate turret until you make it up again!'

Enid Stevens, the last of the best loved child-friends, ranking with Alice Liddell, Gertrude Chataway, Isa Bowman and perhaps one or two others, was scarcely too old for one of the impromptu stories about the strange beasts on the De Morgan tiles round his hearth, for one of the toys out of his big cupboard—Bob the Bat, Leotard, a musical box with the drum put in backwards, or the orguinette with his favourite tune of 'Santa Lucia'—or for the latest game or logical puzzle, when he went for his usual Christmas holiday with his sisters at Guildford in 1897. His last visitors at Oxford were his nieces Menella and Violet, who came to the last of his little select dinner parties on December 17, a few days before he left.

At Guildford he began the new year working hard at the second part of *Symbolic Logic*, but on January 5 he was suffering from a feverish cold. On the eighth he wrote his last letter, No. 98,721 in his Letter Register, and retired to bed. The bronchial symptoms increased, and the end drew suddenly near. 'Take away those pillows,' he said on the 13th, 'I shall need them no more,' and he sank into the sleep which merged into death at 2.30 p.m. on January 14, 1898, with the quiet resignation of the good Christian who had done his best, left the world happier by works which are among its most precious literary heritages, and gone in the full certainty of faith to seek 'that Wonderland which outstrips all our dreams'.

BIBLIOGRAPHY

Bibliography

There is no complete edition of the works of Lewis Carroll, not even excluding the mathematical and logical writings. In 1937 the Nonesuch Press produced an omnibus volume (revised edition 1949) called *The Complete Works of Lewis Carroll*; though in no sense complete, this contains many items either out of print or hard to find. In 1965 Paul Hamlyn Ltd published a fuller volume, *The Works of Lewis Carroll*, of which I was the Editor—but even this is not as complete as might be wished, omitting much of the contents of the early 'family magazines' and *La Guida di Bragia* for reasons of copyright, and the *Alice* variants and junior logic volumes for reasons of space.

In the following Book List an asterisk marks all the items in the Nonesuch volume and a dagger all items added in the Hamlyn edition, which includes the complete Nonesuch volume and a few small items not hitherto collected. I have not tried to list every one of his works, omitting leaflets of purely topical interest and most of his mathematical writings.

I. BOOKS IN PROSE
AND VERSE BY LEWIS CARROLL

*Alice's Adventures in Wonderland. Illustrated by John Tenniel, 1865

†*Bruno's Revenge.* In *Aunt Judy's Magazine*, December 1867. Reprinted in *Modern Fairy Stories* (Dent's Children's Illustrated Classics). Illustrated by E. H. Shepard, 1955

†*Phantasmagoria, and Other Poems*, 1869

*Through the Looking-Glass, and What Alice Found There. Illustrated by John Tenniel, 1872

*The Hunting of the Snark. Illustrated by Henry Holiday, 1876

*Rhyme? And Reason? Illustrated by Arthur Burdett Frost and Henry Holiday, 1883

*_A Tangled Tale._ Illustrated by Arthur Burdett Frost, 1885

Alice's Adventures Underground. Facsimile of the original story, in Dodgson's writing and with his own illustrations, 1886; 1965

*_Alice's Adventures and Through the Looking-Glass._ Illustrated by John Tenniel, 1887. Edition of 1911 contains sixteen of the illustrations completed and coloured by Tenniel. There have been many editions of the two Alices with Tenniel's illustrations; the best are (uncoloured) in Macmillan's St Martin's Library (3/6) and in the Nonesuch Cygnets (30/-) and (coloured, though not Tenniel's colouring) in Dent's Children's Illustrated Classics (12/6)

The Nursery Alice. Twenty coloured enlargements from Tenniel's illustrations, with a new text 'adapted to nursery readers' by Lewis Carroll, 1889; 1966

*_Sylvie and Bruno._ Illustrated by Harry Furniss, 1889

*_Eight or Nine Wise Words About Letter-Writing,_ 1890

*_Sylvie and Bruno Concluded._ Illustrated by Harry Furniss, 1893

*_Three Sunsets, and Other Poems._ Pictures by E. Gertrude Thomson, 1898

†_The Lewis Carroll Picture Book._ Edited by S. Dodgson Collingwood, 1899

The Story of Sylvie and Bruno. Illustrated by Harry Furniss, 1904

†_Feeding the Mind,_ a lecture, 1907

The Rectory Umbrella, and _Mischmasch_ [1849-62], 1932

*_The Collected Verse of Lewis Carroll_ (with the original illustrations), 1932

A Selection of Letters from Lewis Carroll to his Child-friends, 1933

†_The Russian Journal, and Other Selections_ (New York), 1935

The Diaries of Lewis Carroll. Edited by Roger Lancelyn Green, 1953

Useful and Instructive Poetry [1845], 1954

The Book of Nonsense. Edited by Roger Lancelyn Green. (Containing _The Hunting of the Snark,_ many humorous poems, selections from letters to child-friends, etc.) Dent's Children's Illustrated Classics, 1956

BIBLIOGRAPHY

II. ORIGINAL GAMES
AND PUZZLES BY LEWIS CARROLL
[or anonymous]

*Rules for Court Circular, 1860
*Croquet Castles : A Game for Five Players, 1863
Castle-Croquet : A Game for Four Players, 1866
*The Alphabet Cipher, 1868
The Telegraph Cipher, 1868
*Puzzles from Wonderland (in Aunt Judy's Magazine) (December), 1870
*Doublets—A Word Puzzle, 1879
†Lanrick: A Game for Two Players, 1881
*Misch-Masch: A word Game, 1882
*A Tangled Tale. Illustrated by Arthur Burdett Frost, 1885
The Game of Logic, 1886
Memoria Technica, 1888
Circular Billiards for Two Players, 1890
The Wonderland Postage Stamp Case. Four illustrations by John Tenniel, 1890
*A Postal Problem, 1891
*Syzygies, A Word Puzzle, 1891
†A Logical Paradox, 1894
*What the Tortoise Said to Achilles [Logical Puzzle], 1894
Symbolic Logic, Part I, Elementary, 1896

III. SELECT OXFORD AND
MATHEMATICAL PIECES BY CHARLES L. DODGSON
[or anonymous]

*Notes by an Oxford Chiel, containing the pamphlets New Method of Evaluation of π (1865), Dynamics of a Particle (1865), Facts, Figures and Fancies (1866-8), The New Belfry (1872), The Vision of the Three T's (1873), The Blank Cheque (1874). All these are humorous works, satirising University or Christ Church subjects, 1874
Euclid and his Modern Rivals, 1879
*Lawn Tennis Tournaments, 1883

The Principles of Parliamentary Representation, 1884
Four Pamphlets on Parliamentary Representation. Reprinted in
Duncan Black's *The Theory of Committees and Elections*, 1958

IV. MISCELLANEOUS
ITEMS BY LEWIS CARROLL

**Some Popular Fallacies about Vivisection*, 1875
†*An Easter Greeting to every child who loves 'Alice'*, 1876
†*Alice on the Stage* (in *The Theatre*). [Essay], April, 1887
†*The Stage and the Spirit of Reverence* (in *The Theatre*). [Essay],
    July 1888
†*Children's Sermon* (in *St Mary Magdalen Parish Magazine*,
    St Leonards), November, 1897
†*The Legend of Scotland* (story written January 1858), 1899
†*Isa's Visit to Oxford* (written for Isa Bowman, July 1888), 1899
    [The last five of these are included in *The Lewis Carroll Picture
    Book*—1899]
†*Crundle Castle* (story in *The Rectory Magazine*—1848), 1953
Mr C. and Mr T. (puzzle-story remembered orally by a child-
    friend, Mary Burrows [Mrs Knyvett]), 1953
    [The last two were first published in *The Diaries of Lewis
    Carroll* (1953), which also contains many verses and letters
    hitherto unpublished or uncollected]

V. BOOKS ABOUT LEWIS CARROLL

The Life and Letters of Lewis Carroll, by S. Dodgson Colling-
    wood, 1898
The Story of Lewis Carroll, by Isa Bowman, 1899
A Handbook of the Literature of the Rev. C. L. Dodgson, by
    S. H. Williams and Falconer Madan, 1931 (supplement added
    in 1935). Revised, augmented and brought up to date as
    The Lewis Carroll Handbook by Roger Lancelyn Green (1962)
The Life of Lewis Carroll, by Langford Reed, 1932
The Lewis Carroll Centenary in London, by Falconer Madan, 1932
Carroll's Alice, by Harry Morgan Ayres [New York], 1936
Victoria Through the Looking-Glass, by Florence Becker Lennon
    [New York], 1945

[The same, in England, as *Lewis Carroll: A Biography*, 1947, Cassell]. Revised edition, New York, 1962

The Story of Lewis Carroll, by Roger Lancelyn Green, Methuen, 1949

Lewis Carroll: Photographer, by Helmut Gernsheim, Parrish, 1949

The White Knight: A Study of C. L. Dodgson, by Alexander L. Taylor, Oliver and Boyd, 1952

Lewis Carroll, by Derek Hudson, Constable, 1954

Swift and Carroll, by Phyllis Greenacre, M.D. [New York], 1955

Alice in Many Tongues, by Warren Weaver [Wisconsin], 1964

VI. A FEW ARTICLES
AND PAMPHLETS OF SPECIAL INTEREST

Lewis Carroll, by Beatrice Hatch, *Strand Magazine*, April 1898

C. L. Dodgson, by F. York Powell, in Oliver Elton's *Frederick York Powell*, 1906

Recollections of Lewis Carroll, by Harry Furniss, *Strand Magazine*, January 1908

Reminiscences of Lewis Carroll, by Ethel M. Arnold, *Windsor Magazine*, December 1929

Lewis Carroll, by Walter de la Mare, *The Eighteen-Eighties*, 1930, separately 1932

Alice's Recollections of Carrollian Days, *Cornhill Magazine*, July 1932

Alice: The Child as Swain, in *Some versions of Pastoral*, by William Empson, 1935

Logic and the Humour of Lewis Carroll, by Peter Alexander, Leeds, May 1951

Lewis Carroll's Periodical Publications, by Roger Lancelyn Green, in *Notes and Queries*, March 1954

Lewis Carroll, by Derek Hudson [*Writers and their Work*, No. 96], British Council, 1958

The Theory of Committees and Elections (Section xx and Appendix), by Duncan Black, 1958

E. Nesbit

ANTHEA BELL

ACKNOWLEDGMENTS

There have been two books written about E. Nesbit. *E. Nesbit: A Biography*, by Doris Langley Moore (Cassell) gives a fascinating picture of E. Nesbit's life, her family and her friends. *Magic and the Magician*, by Noel Streatfeild (Benn) throws new light on her childhood. I am very much indebted to both books.

My grateful thanks are due to:

Miss Janet Hill, Children's Librarian of Lambeth.

Mr John Denton, of Ernest Benn Ltd, who publish E. Nesbit's children's books.

Mr Innes Rose, of John Farquharson Ltd, who handle her work and gave me permission to quote from her autobiographical writings.

Mr Roger Lancelyn Green, who very kindly drew my attention to and lent me magazine articles containing E. Nesbit's reminiscences of childhood, now published in book form as *Long Ago When I Was Young* (Whiting & Wheaton).

CONTENTS

1. Introduction

On August 15th, 1858, a second daughter was born to Sarah and John Collis Nesbit. The baby was named Edith, but her pet name in the family was Daisy; forty years later she was to become known to the juvenile reading public as E. Nesbit. Succeeding generations of children having ratified the judgment of this first public, her immortality must now be assured in that particular corner of the literary field where she rather surprisingly made her name at last.

In 1858, her father, an agricultural chemist of considerable repute, was running an agricultural college in Lower Kennington Lane. There was a small farm attached to the college for practical work—'Fancy a farm in Kennington!' wrote E. Nesbit in 1896. During the nineteenth century this part of London was fast becoming a built-up area, but as well as the farm there was space for a garden and a meadow for the Nesbit family. The metropolis was changing rapidly in E. Nesbit's own life-time; the present-day reader must adjust his ideas even more drastically to envisage the almost pastoral character of her birthplace in Lower Kennington Lane. Her stories for children are essentially timeless, though their characters are Edwardian, but her own childhood must be set firmly in the mid-Victorian period, and it is from her own childhood that her books really spring.

What was that period like for a child actually growing up in it? It is a far cry from the anxiety-ridden parental permissiveness of today to family life of the Victorian era, when family life was a formidable institution in itself.

Family life meant security, order, tradition, the means to 'train up a child in the way he should go'. Emphasis was laid on the spiritual benefits to be got by learning a proper submission to Authority. As for the family itself, it would probably be large, and father very much the head of it—legendary and tyrannical Victorian father, with invalid Victorian mother, the victim of constant pregnancies, reclining exhausted upon her sofa.

Of course there was another side to the coin, as to all clichés that ever have been coined. Not even the sternest *paterfamilias* always got his own way. Edmund Gosse had a particularly puritanical father, who tried to wean his son from worldly frivolity by suggesting that an invitation to a children's party should be 'laid before the Lord', thus indicating just what he thought the Lord's advice should be. To the consternation of Gosse senior, the small boy rebelled, replying 'in the high-piping accents of despair: "The Lord says I may go to the Browns" '. The importance of Nurse in the middle-class family might make for less intimacy between mother and child, but there were always mothers like Mrs Trollope who, undeterred by frequent child-bearing and the consequent rearing of weak children, could cope with family problems and inadequate husbands, and still make a reasonable amount of money from their own writings. E. Nesbit's own mother was possessed of energy and determination enough to make her try to run the agricultural college after her husband's death, and deal with the problems attendant upon travel on the Continent with her three daughters. Many parents, like Mrs Nesbit, were obviously congenial companions to their large, lively families, and much beloved by them. The children themselves, seen and not heard in the drawing-room, had their own domain in the nursery. If there was not much ready-made entertainment available, there were many ways for children to entertain themselves, especially in a large family. The correspondence columns of *Aunt Judy's Magazine*, founded by Mrs Gatty in 1865 and edited by her until her death in 1873, give one a cross-section of their amusements and activities. They ask Aunt Judy for scraps of information, answers to riddles, names of suitable plays for family performance. They enjoy keeping pets, advertising guinea-pigs or white mice, wanted and for sale.

'"E.M.B." offers four tame rabbits, young, and prettily marked.'

'Can our readers supply "B.E.B." with some hints on the rearing of young doves? Three successive broods have died under her care, and she fears that the losses must have been due to mismanagement.'

'"Maud" will be grateful to any reader who will give her some silkworms' eggs.'

And 'Madge', a more advanced silkworm keeper, writes to ask 'where she can sell her silkworms' silk'.

There are the collectors, who write offering to exchange birds' eggs, mosses, and so forth:

'"E.H.B." will be glad to know of any place where she can send well-mounted specimens of seaweeds and albums containing sets of prettily arranged specimens, to sell.'

'"Wee Mull" will be glad to know where she can obtain a death's head moth.'

A grisly little incident seems to lie behind Aunt Judy's reply to 'A Young Naturalist'.

'If camphor fails to keep your *Lepidoptera* in good condition, Aunt Judy thinks that some mistake must have been made in the preservation of your specimens. All *thick-bodied* ones should have their insides removed, and be lined with cotton wool.'

There is much trafficking in pincushions and similar bits of handicraft earnestly made in order to earn money for good works.

To one high-minded girl Aunt Judy writes,

'You had better ask some learned friend to guide you in your study of Metaphysics, otherwise you will merely dabble at the outermost edge of the subject and learn nothing. . . . I do not think that a *general* catalogue of fossils with illustrations has been published. . . . The best small book on coins of which I can tell you is Humphreys' "Coin Collector's Manual".'

Books enter into the negotiations between Aunt Judy's readers.

'"Welda" wishes to obtain a Persian or a Russian kitten, and offers story-books in exchange, such as "Christie Redfern's Troubles"; "Lizzie Hepburn"; or "Every Cloud has a Silver Lining".'

Aunt Judy's Magazine was a sign of the times; in the nineteenth century, when family life meant so much, there was a growing interest in children and concern about their welfare, even including their amusement. One result was the rise and popularity of books to entertain children as well as to inform and edify them—and so arose the classics of a new kind of literature, aimed at a new and appreciative reading public.

When E. Nesbit herself came to write for this newly recognised juvenile public, she wrote stories that hardly date at all. They have not even the slight quaintness a child today may find in some of the best Victorian children's writers. It seems almost a significant coincidence that she began writing for children at the turn of the century, the end of the Victorian era. But in fact, there was nothing we think of as conventionally Victorian even about the first forty years of E. Nesbit's life. She was one of a large, affectionate family, but for most of her childhood the Nesbits were moving from place to place, and had no settled home. Nor did she find security as a young married woman. Her own outlook on life was not at all what we would consider Victorian; her sympathies were with the newer, more adventurous trends of thought prevailing towards the end of the nineteenth century.

It would be a mistake, too, to assume that books written in the first decade of the twentieth century—as most of E. Nesbit's work for children was—would necessarily feel more 'modern' than strictly Victorian books. She wrote for children of sixty years ago who would now have grand-children of an age to read E. Nesbit for themselves. A great many ways of thought, conventions and restrictions lingered on from the last century. In *The Story of the Amulet* Cyril, a boy from the present brought before an Ancient Egyptian Pharaoh, tries to impress him with some resounding phrases culled from the newspaper about the empire where the sun never sets, while he belongs to 'the great Anglo-Saxon or conquering race'—a notion engendered by a hundred years of peace from Waterloo to the outbreak of the 1914 War, broken only by the minor forays of the Crimean and Boer Wars. It is hard today to realise what a safe place the world could seem.

Suppose a child were now transported back sixty years by amulet—like Cyril and his brother and sisters in the story— he would find features of this safe Edwardian world very strange to him. It would be a place where nursery-maids and cooks were kept as a matter of course; where he could buy sweets for a penny an ounce; where little girls were burdened with hats and petticoats and stockings all the year round. He would find hansom-cabs and horse-buses in the streets—motor-cars would be something to stare at. And instead of petrol-stations he would see loads of straw and fodder as he went through the city streets.

But one thing he would *not* find strange. The children, in spite of their odd clothes, would be very much like himself. He still enjoys the books E. Nesbit wrote for and about such children. Her books are modern—or rather, timeless—because the children in them ring true to childhood of any time. She does not do it by removing her characters to a dateless nonsense world or fantasy world of their own; when the most remarkable and magical things happen to them, they happen against a background of everyday life in that world now sixty years away in time and even further by any other measure of change. Any but the very best children's books of that time are now period pieces.

II. E. Nesbit—The Child

Edith Nesbit was the youngest of her family. Her eldest sister, Saretta, was the daughter of Mrs Nesbit's first marriage. The next sister, Mary, a delicate girl, was also much older than Edith. But although they were too grown-up to be playmates for the child, they were evidently very fond of her. E. Nesbit remembered Saretta as a kind elder sister with a gift for telling fairy-stories. Once, in France, Saretta thought to gratify her small sister by taking her to see a real shepherdess, but Edith, expecting to meet a beautiful creature in silks and ribbons out of one of these fairy-tales, was bitterly disappointed to find only a wrinkled, kindly old woman. Saretta and Mary, too, took her to see the 'mummies' at Bordeaux, a collection of corpses preserved by the earth of the churchyard. Unfortunately this was not a success—all three had expected to find mummies neatly bound and encased as in the British Museum, and the sight of 'skeletons with the flesh hardened on their bones, with their long dry hair hanging on each side of the brown faces' shocked and terrified Edith.

However, there must have been more cheerful expeditions arranged by Mary and Saretta for their small sister. Of a holiday in Brittany she writes,

'My eldest sister was always a refuge on wet days when a fairy-story seemed to be the best thing to be had.

In the midst of all the parties, picnics and gaieties in which our elders were plunged, my other sister found time to read aloud to us, and to receive such confidences as we deemed it wise to make concerning our plans and plays.'

'We' were Edith and her two brothers, Alfred and Henry. The boys, being much nearer in age than her sisters, were her companions and fellow-conspirators. They figure large in her memories of childhood.

For the first four years of E. Nesbit's life, everything seemed to promise that this childhood would be a happily settled, uneventful one. But two things happened to change it, the first her father's death in 1862, the second her sister Mary's ill-health. Between them they uprooted the family first from London, then from England, whence Mrs Nesbit took her children to the Continent, moving around to any place which she thought might do Mary's health good.

E. Nesbit herself wrote a series of articles in the *Girl's Own Paper* of 1896-1897 about those early years, recently published as *Long Ago When I Was Young*, illustrated by Edward Ardizzone (Whiting & Wheaton, 1966). Their pattern was one of constantly changing schools in term-time, in the holidays a nomadic life in France. None of the many schools Edith attended was a success. Of the one she liked best, run by a Mrs MacBean, all she could say was, 'If I could have been happy at any school, I should have been happy there.' Misery at school, rapture on being re-united with her family, are recurrent themes. At her first school, in Brighton, where the Nesbit family was living at the time, she encountered an unpleasant child who bullied her and spoiled her toys, and when Edith protested, threatened,

'"If you say a word about it I'll say you did it and pinched me as well. And Mrs Arthur'll believe me, because I'm not a new girl, and you are."'

This was probably the first time Edith had met feminine malice—her brothers teased her, but were not intentionally unkind—and it made her feel desolate. To make matters worse, the unattainable refuge of home was actually before her eyes. Although she went home on Saturdays, she still felt homesick when she passed her house on school walks.

Her next school, in Stamford, was no improvement. This time the trouble was her untidiness and inability to do compound long division. She was always being punished— nursing 'an indignant sense that I could do sums well enough if anyone would tell me what they meant'. When she learned that her mother and sisters were going to France, she begged to go too. Mrs Nesbit, seeing how unhappy she was at the Stamford school, took her away, and the family's wanderings in France began.

If she was unlucky in her schools, Edith was very fortunate in having a sympathetic mother. Mrs Nesbit was affectionate and understanding, rather indulgent, perhaps, to her youngest daughter, even by present-day standards. When the Nesbits were living near Dinan, Edith was sent to a school in the town. By mistake she arrived a few days before term started, and was so bored and miserable that she ran all the way home. 'I think my mother must have understood something of what I went through,' she writes, 'for she did not send me back.'

Edith's other schools included a French convent school, where the nuns found her high spirits rather alarming, and a German school, which she disliked so heartily that she tried to run away and find her brothers at their school (also in Germany) no less than three times.

The happiest time she spent away from her family was her three months in Pau with a French family. There she lived in a home-like atmosphere, not breathing the more impersonal air of a boarding-school. The little girl, Marguerite, became great friends with Edith, though she was not such a kindred spirit as Alfred and Henry, being more matter-of-fact than the Nesbit children with their inventive imaginations. Was she, perhaps, in part the original of Madeline? One day the two girls put the cat in a hamper, to play the part of a captive princess. They were called away in the middle of their game, and forgot the cat for three days. Edith suddenly remembered her in the middle of the night.

'It was winter; the snow was on the ground. Marguerite thoughtfully put on her shoes and her dressing-gown, but I, with some vague recollection of bare-footed pilgrims, and some wild desire to make expiation for my crime, went down bare-footed, in my night-gown. . . . We crept through the house like mice; across the courtyard, thinly sprinkled with snow, and into that awful black yawning cellar where nameless horrors lurked behind each bit of shapeless lumber, ready to leap out upon us as we passed. Marguerite did not share my terrors. She only remarked that it was very cold and that we must make haste.'

The cat, to Edith's great relief, was alive.

'Nameless horrors' played quite a large part in E. Nesbit's childhood. She was a sensitive, temperamental child, prone to strong emotions—fear, unhappiness, longing for home—that blotted everything else from her horizon. She tormented herself with her vivid imagination, and kept her torments to herself, rather than go to an adult for comfort.

'One used to lie awake in the silence, listening, listening to the pad-pad of one's own heart, straining one's ears to make sure that it was not the pad-pad of something else, something unspeakable creeping towards one out of the horrible dense dark.'

In this frame of mind, she could lie awake all night because what her reason *knew* to be only a dress on a bed, in the dim light of gas turned low, figured in her imagination as a corpse and a skeleton. On the journey from England to France, she had a nightmare about her father's ghost, which she describes as 'the first remembrance I have of any terror of the dead or of the supernatural'. It was induced, with the apparent inconsequence of such workings of the mind, by

'a horror of the words *Débit de Tabac* which I had noticed on our way from the station; I associated them with the gravestone of my father, I don't know why, I can only conjecture that the last syllable of *Débit* being the same as that of our name, may have had something to do with it.'

Mrs Nesbit could rescue her daughter from the miseries of school at Stamford, but not the most loving mother could guard against this kind of thing. Even the 'crowning horror', as E. Nesbit described it, of the mummies of Bordeaux, could not have been anticipated—indeed, she had begged to go and see them.

But these horrors did not overshadow her young life all the time. They generally attacked in the dark, when she was alone. In daylight, playing with her brothers, she was quite carefree. In spite of her fear of the mummies and her father's grave, she could revel in the macabre on occasion, like most children. When the family were in Poitiers, she picked up a bone in a churchyard and cherished it.

'It was human, I was convinced, and I wove many romances round the little brown relic—romances that considerably embittered the reality when I came to know it.

"What's that?" Alfred asked, picking the bone from its resting-place in cotton-wool in my corner drawer months afterwards.

"A human bone," I said gravely.

Alfred roared with aggravating laughter.

"It's only half a fowl's back—you little silly."

Ashamed and confused I flung the bone back into the inmost recesses of the drawer, and assured him that he was mistaken. But he wasn't.'

This is more like the imagined children of E. Nesbit's own stories—ever romantically hopeful, but with a brother or sister always at hand to do some debunking when necessary.

Her childhood was an eventful one by the standards of today, let alone by those of Victoria's reign. Once Mrs Nesbit and the three girls travelled through the mountains of Auvergne in a hired carriage which, despite Mrs Nesbit's protests, kept filling up with the driver's relations. First his stepson, then father, brother-in-law, uncle and cousin joined the party. The Englishwomen began to fear they would be robbed.

' "If we only get to the half-way house," she (Mrs Nesbit) said, "we can appeal to the landlord for protection," and after a seemingly interminable drive we got to the half-way house.

It was a low, roughly-built, dirty auberge, with an uneven, earthen floor, the ceiling, benches and tables black with age, just the place where travellers are always murdered in Christmas stories. My teeth chattered with terror, but there was a certain pleasure in the excitement all the same. . . . When the woman brought in our bill, my mother poured out her woes and confessed her fear of the driver's intention.

"Nonsense," said the woman briskly, "he's the best man in the world—he's my own son! Surely he has a right to give his own relations a lift in his carriage if he likes!" '

But adventures such as this, and the Nesbits' constant journeys from one town of France to another, did not particularly appeal to the child. She missed the settled home life that most children had as a permanent background. When the family did establish itself in a house for any length of time, she seized eagerly on the joys of being 'at home'.

'I was bored with travel,' she writes, 'as I believe all children are—so large a part of a child's life is made up of little familiar playthings and objects; it has little of that historic and artistic sense which lends colour and delight to travel.'

Especially she loved the house near Dinan in Brittany which Mrs Nesbit took one summer. She remembers her arrival from Mrs MacBean's school in England.

'A long drive on a diligence by miles and miles of straight white road—the fatigue of the journey forgotten in the consciousness that I was going home, not to an hotel, not to a boarding-house, but home.

The small material objects that surround one's daily life have always influenced me deeply. Even as a child I found that in a familiar *entourage* one could be contented, if not happy; but hotels and boarding-houses and lodgings have always bored me to extinction.'

This house at Dinan she called 'the dearest home of my childhood', and she describes it in loving detail. Here she, Alfred and Henry spent 'an ideally happy' summer. Their mother, again with indulgent understanding beyond what one expects in the usual idea of a Victorian parent, let them be free to do just as they liked. They explored the surrounding country, enjoyed the resources of the house and the farm buildings, ate cherries in the orchard. On wet days, besides Saretta's fairy stories, there was a hayloft to play in.

'With trusses of hay or straw, a magnificent fort could be made. I usually held the fort when the boys had built it, and the weakness of the garrison was lessened by the introduction of the two dogs, who defended it with me nobly, understanding perfectly the parts they had to play. We got the black pig up once, but that was a failure.'

Readers of *The Wouldbegoods* will remember the uncooperative black pig that refused to play its part in a circus. And in this holiday at Dinan lay the seeds of more than one of the Bastables' exploits. Between Edith and her brothers there was just the same sort of family feeling that she put down on paper many years later when she created that famous family. In this part of her reminiscences, which she labelled *Pirates and Explorers*, one sees the Nesbit/Bastable imagination at work thinking up exciting games. This was the beginning of the pirate game.

'There was a delightful pond in the field where the farm horses went to drink. It had a trampled muddy shore on one side, and on the other a high bank of yellow clay. We made a raft, of course, out of an old door and two barrels, and successfully sailed across to the yellow cliffs.

"How nice it would be," I said, "if there were a cave in those cliffs; we could have no end of a good time and be pirates and things."

"You don't suppose," said Alfred scornfully, "that a pirate chief would wait to find a cave if he wanted one—he would make one of course."

"I don't believe you can," said Harry and I in a breath.

"All right," said my brother, "you'll see!"

Next morning, when Harry and I went out into the field, there was Alfred, ankle deep in water, shovelling out clay from the banks.

"What a big hole you've made," said I. "I believe I could get into it if I curled up very much."

"Ah!" said my brother grimly, "you thought I couldn't do it."

"Do you mean to say you aren't going to let us go shares," said Harry, reading his brother's tone instantly.

"Not a share," said Alfred firmly, "this is going to be my cave, and if I find anyone in it without my leave, I'll throw him to the alligators."

"There aren't any alligators," said Harry, "there are only ducks," and indeed there were several swimming about the yellow waters of the pond.

"All right," said Alfred cheerfully, sending a large spadeful of clay splashing into the pond, "I'll throw you to the ducks then. I daresay they'll do just as well." '

But peace was finally made. Edith and Harry walked into the town to buy a large green sugar-stick for a peace-offering. Alfred reacted like a true Bastable prototype (' "You little duffers . . . I don't want your *sucre de pomme*, I only wanted you to say you were sorry" ') and thereafter all three enjoyed the pirate cave.

The fascination of water as a plaything was something E. Nesbit never grew out of. All her life she loved boating and swimming. In Brittany there was a stream to explore as well as a pond—a stream that turns up again to be explored in *The Wouldbegoods*. Edith and her brother had made a similar expedition.

'We built dams and bridges . . . we caught fish with butterfly nets in the sandy shallows; we called it the Nile and pretended that there were crocodiles in it, and that the rocks among the woods were temples and pyramids.

One day Alfred proposed that we should try and find the source of it. . . .

"I think we ought to wade up," said Alfred, "there are no crocodiles in this part of the river, but the lions and tigers on the banks are something awful."

So we waded up stream, which was tiring work, let me tell you.

"I don't see a single lion," I said presently, "but I'm sure I saw a crocodile just now under that bank."

So we got out and walked by the stream's edge on the short, fine, sun-warmed turf. . . . With a thrill of delight we saw that the water ran from a little brick tunnel, the mouth of which was draped in a green veil of maidenhair. I suppose it was about four feet high.

"You'll turn back now," said Harry triumphantly.

For all answer, Alfred stooped and plunged into the darkness of the little tunnel. I followed, and Harry brought up the rear.'

The outbreak of the Franco-Prussian War in 1870 brought the Nesbit family's travels to an end, and delivered Edith from the German school where she was at the time. The family returned to England, and Mrs Nesbit bought a house with a large garden at Halstead in Kent. This was the first permanent home Edith had known since the days of the Kennington agricultural college, and she loved it. There was a pond (with a raft, of course), there was a door leading on to the roof, where the children 'kept a store of books and good things' in their secret place between the 'four pointed roofs of tiles'. There was a shrubbery where Edith could lose herself with a book—and in her own room there was a desk where she could sit and write poetry, locking the door against her brothers. While the Nesbits were still at Halstead, she had some verses accepted by a magazine for the first time.

III. E. Nesbit—The Woman

In the late '70s, owing to some financial difficulties, the family left Halstead and came to live in London. Edith, who had so enjoyed the pleasant country life, thought nostalgically of Halstead during her years in London, and sometimes made sentimental pilgrimages back there.

She was now a young woman, with ambitions to become a poet. At about this time she met her future husband, Hubert Bland. She married him at a registry office, in 1880. Their married life was to be long and difficult; the fact that, all things considered, it was a successful marriage, was due mainly to Edith's own remarkable strength of character.

Quite soon after the Blands had settled down in a small house in Lewisham, the first of the trials that were to bring out this strength of character presented themselves. Hubert Bland and a partner had started a small business for manufacturing brushes. Bland caught small-pox, and was dangerously ill; when he recovered, it was only to find that while he was ill his partner had absconded with all the capital of the business. He was still a convalescent, the couple already had a baby, and Edith had to earn money for the family by whatever means she could. This was not easy in the days when most gentlewomen were not trained to meet such an emergency; fortunately there was a certain market for the usual accomplishments of the Victorian young lady. Edith painted decorative cards for sale (it was an added advantage that she could make up her own verses to go on the cards), and gave recitations.

But she had, of course, a particular talent of her own.

She had already had some work printed in magazines; now she took seriously to her pen as a commercial proposition. For the next fifteen or twenty years she wrote copiously, anything and everything that would sell. She wrote love-stories, horror-stories, verses, novels, even some work for children (contributing, for example, to collections with titles like *Sunny Tales for Snowy Days*, *Tales That Are True for Brown Eyes and Blue*). Astonishingly, nothing in her vast output at this time really foreshadowed what was to come.

She was a woman of great energy, one of those people who seem to cram twice as much into their time as ordinary beings. In the years after her marriage, she not only kept house on a small budget, wrote, painted and recited to earn money for the household, bore and brought up her children, but she found room for other interests as well. The Blands held progressive views. Edith shocked the conventional by wearing her hair short, smoking cigarettes, and dressing herself and her daughters in unfashionably loose, flowing clothes according to the aesthetic *avant-garde* of the day. She and her husband became active Socialists, and were founder members of the Fabian Society. Hubert Bland took the chair at its first meeting. He himself had begun to write after his illness, at first collaborating with Edith in stories for magazines. He had now become a journalist, and he was a prominent figure in the Fabian Society all his life.

The Blands' house became something of a social centre for their fellow Fabians. They adored entertaining their friends, and were always generously hospitable, whether they could afford it or not. Among the friends they made at this time was Bernard Shaw. One feels that E. Nesbit probably liked best this personal aspect of the Fabian Society—the circle of lively, unconventional friends it brought her. She seems to have been content to let her

husband mould her opinions on most political subjects.
Hubert Bland, progressive as he was in theory, was opposed
to women's suffrage; so, therefore, was Edith, though one
would have thought it just the cause to appeal to a woman of
her character and views. But then, Hubert Bland was a
political journalist, and ideas were his *métier*; his wife was a
writer of stories, and people and events were hers. When it
came to putting socialist ideas into practice, she threw
herself enthusiastically into social work. She organised
outings for the poor children of Deptford, and Christmas
parties on a large scale, lavishly charitable both of her
money and her time.

One great pleasure of hers was the boating holidays the
Blands would sometimes take with friends. Then she would
revel whole-heartedly in swimming, rowing and leading an
active outdoor life. Indeed, whatever she did was done
whole-heartedly; once any enthusiasm had taken hold of her,
she did not lightly forsake it. (In later life, she spent a great
deal of time and energy trying to prove that Bacon wrote the
works of Shakespeare, by a system of logarithms which she
did not really understand.) She had an amazing zest for living, which bore her up through the struggles of her early
married life. This itself was not by any means a smooth-
running affair. Hubert Bland was not intended by nature for
a monogamist, and his wife had a good deal to put up with.
There were occasional bitter quarrels; but Edith brought up
two of his children with her own. As a mother herself, she
was not ideal. She lacked the stable, understanding temperament of her own mother, and was a little haphazard, if
charming, in her attitude to her children. She could not
understand, for instance, that her daughters would rather
look like everyone else than be dressed in the 'aesthetic'
clothes they wore—a curious failure of imagination in

someone who had the youth of spirit to invent the Bastable family at the age of forty.

In volumes of *Nister's Holiday Annual* of 1894-1896 there appeared a story by E. Nesbit called *The Play Times* which showed the beginnings of the Bastable style, and was the original idea of the chapter 'Being Editors' in *The Story of the Treasure Seekers*. In 1896-1897 she wrote the series of articles for the *Girl's Own Paper* which recalled so vividly her own childhood. In 1898 the Bastable stories began to appear in the *Pall Mall Magazine* and the *Windsor Magazine*, and the next year they were published in book form. This was the usual procedure with her books—they appeared first in serial form in magazines, mostly in the *Strand Magazine*, before being issued as books. E. Nesbit had at last found her true vein. It brought her prosperity. Hubert Bland, too, was now well established as a journalist, and the Blands moved to a large country house, Well Hall in Kent, where they lived for the next twenty-three years. Edith put this house in several of her books; it is the Moat House of *The Wouldbegoods*.

The Blands were no longer struggling, but there was no slackening of Edith's energy. She continued to write short stories, poetry and novels, while she produced regularly during the next fourteen years the children's books for which she is remembered. While she was still engaged on the story of the Bastables in *The Treasure Seekers* and its two sequels, *The Wouldbegoods* and *New Treasure Seekers*, she began her first series of fantasies, *Five Children and It*, *The Phoenix and the Carpet* and *The Story of the Amulet*. She returned to a story of real life without magic in *The Railway Children* and followed it by another fantasy, *The Enchanted Castle*, and then by two semi-historical stories, *The House of Arden* and *Harding's Luck*. In 1910 *The Magic City* was published.

This is not one of E. Nesbit's best books, but it is interesting to a student of her work because it was based on a game she used to play for her own children, of building cities out of ordinary objects lying about the house—the kind that Philip and his grown-up sister Helen in the book use—

'Boxes of bricks and certain other things in the house—her Japanese cabinet, the dominoes and chessmen, cardboard boxes, books, the lids of kettles and teapots.'

She was invited to build one of these cities at the Children's Welfare Exhibition at Olympia in 1912, an invitation which shows how well-known and popular she had become as a children's author. *The Magic City* was followed by *The Wonderful Garden*, a collection of stories, *The Magic World*, and *Wet Magic*.

E. Nesbit's early years at Well Hall, in particular, were happy ones. She could follow all her hospitable inclinations, and entertained with Bohemian informality. She loved especially to invite talented young authors, artists and politicians—many of whom afterwards became famous—to Well Hall. She also had a cottage at Dymchurch, and here too she would invite her friends. It was at Dymchurch that she first met H. G. Wells, who left his own impressions of the Bland household in his *Experiment in Autobiography*.

She was always ready to begin some new enterprise; in 1907 she became joint editor of a new quarterly, printed by lithography, called *The Neolith*. To this quarterly she devoted a good deal of time during its brief life of four numbers. At about the same time she took up the cause of Bacon. She was always ready, too, to be interested in other people, and wrote some charming letters to children who admired her books. She had assumed the style of Oswald, who tells the Bastable stories, so convincingly that some of them wrote to Oswald as a real person.

As she grew older, difficulties again beset her. Hubert Bland was going blind, and in 1914 he died. Edith went away to France for a short time after her husband's death, and came home very ill. At last the flood of her energy was checked. She had never saved much money, even when she was prosperous, and now she found her financial affairs quite beyond her. She struggled on at Well Hall, taking paying guests in the house through the war years. For the first time in her life, her problems were a depressing burden to bear, not a challenge to be overcome.

Then she made a second marriage, which lifted the burden from her shoulders. Her husband was Thomas Terry Tucker, a marine engineer, a widower who had been a friend of the Blands for some years. They were married in 1917. He was a capable and cheerful man, and E. Nesbit was very happy with him.

In 1921 they left Well Hall, and went to live in a bungalow not far from Dymchurch. Here she spent the last four years of her life. Tucker had persuaded her to begin writing for children again, and she wrote the stories that were to appear posthumously as *Five of Us—And Madeline*. Even in poor health, she kept her liveliness of mind, as these stories, the letters she wrote to friends and the accounts of people who visited her at this time show. She died in May 1924, after a long illness.

There was something rather childlike about E. Nesbit all her life, in her impetuous generosity, her love of making a grand gesture, her fits of temper and sensitivity to criticism. But she was tenacious as well as impetuous. There was nothing childish in the strength of character that enabled her to make a success of her career and her marriage. Yet it was the child in E. Nesbit who remembered how it felt to be a small girl playing pirates and explorers with her brothers, and who wrote the books that are still read today.

iv. E. Nesbit—The Writer

It seems extraordinary that E. Nesbit could have written so much, for so long, before striking her own rich vein of story-telling for children. Even when at last she did, she seems not to have realised just how different it was from the rest of her work, mentioning the first stories in a letter to her mother merely as 'a children's book called "The Treasure Seekers".' All her life, E. Nesbit really considered herself a poet *manqué*. She had books of poetry published, and indeed mildly praised; she thought them her most important work. Her verse was facile and in no way out of the ordinary, but she did resent having to spend so much time writing prose instead of being able to devote herself entirely to poetry. Yet unknown to herself and her poetic ambitions, her real gift was the balanced, objective outlook of a comic prose writer. (As a woman, she was always temperamental and fond of dramatising herself, but she disliked putting her feelings down on paper. She remarked on her reluctance to write personal, subjective poetry, 'Right or wrong, I could never bring myself to lay my soul naked before the public. My published poems are nearly all dramatic lyrics.') It was when she began to write for children and draw on her resources of comedy and realism that she at last found herself as a writer.

But the quantities of hack-work E. Nesbit did during her first twenty years of authorship had their uses. By the time she invented Oswald Bastable she was an experienced professional who had learned the technique of story-telling. A great part of her work in those twenty years was short stories. There was a considerable market for them in the magazines of the time, and each one had to have a well-defined plot of its own. It is on record that E. Nesbit used sometimes to ask her friends to think of plots for her, an indication that she was really happier creating characters. In some of her later books for children, the strain of thinking up plots does begin to show. If her children got into difficulties, she would cut the knot of the story by bringing characters out of books by magic to dispose of any enemies. She uses this trick in both *The Magic City* and *Wet Magic*, and the scene at the end of *Harding's Luck* when a crowd of famous heroes and heroines dressed in white urge Edred to be brave is a similar device. It was not a very inspired idea. On the other hand, she was practically never at a loss to create a really lifelike child. And in her best work—the Bastable stories and the first three fantasies—she shows apparently effortless powers of comic invention, quite up to the standard set by the liveliness of the characters.

Another result of E. Nesbit's years of experience as a writer-of-all-trades was that her work for children, seen in the light of other contemporary writing, seems to belong in tone with the adult stories of the time rather than other children's books. Indeed, the Bastable stories made their appearance in magazines where they would be read by adults before being passed on to the children. There was a spirit of jovial comedy in many adult stories of the time—such as one finds, for instance, in Stevenson's *The Wrong Box*—and E. Nesbit took it over into children's books when she invented the Bastables and their well-meant mistakes. As for the fantasies, E. Nesbit's Psammead may owe something to Mrs Molesworth's 'fairyfied cuckoo', which scolds Griselda as the Psammead scolds Cyril and the rest, and

holds similar opinions on Time, described by the Psammead as 'only a mode of thought':

'"And what is slow, and what is quick?" said the cuckoo.
"*All* a matter of fancy! If everything that's been done since
the world was made till now, was done over again in five
minutes, you'd never know the difference".'

The Cuckoo Clock (1877)

Closer, perhaps, come the stories of F. Anstey, who like
E. Nesbit shows magic intruding into everyday life, to the
great embarrassment of the people who encounter it. The
children in *The Story of the Amulet*, trying to deal with an
Ancient Egyptian priest in Edwardian London, are in much
the same predicament as Horace, the young architect hero
of *The Brass Bottle*, who frees an inconveniently grateful
Arabian Nights genie from his bottle prison. Anstey's
books belong in a kind of half-way house—he wrote in the
first instance for adults, but is much enjoyed by children—
and E. Nesbit is in a half-way house only slightly different;
she wrote for children, but adults do not grow out of liking
her books. The humour of incongruity is a strong point
of both writers. The management of a dramatic surprise
such as the routing of the two Cockney lads Urb and Ike
by the Phoenix is something that, one feels, E. Nesbit owes
to her experience as an adult writer.

'"Hearken, O Eikonoclastes, despiser of sacred images—
and thou, Urbanus, dweller in a sordid city. Forbear this
adventure lest a worse thing befall."

"Luv us!" said Ike, "ain't it been taught its schoolin', just."

"Forbear," repeated the Phoenix, sternly. "Who pinched
the click off the old bloke in Aldermanbury?" it added in a
changed tone. "Who sneaked the nose-rag out of the young
gell's 'and in Bell Court?" '

The Phoenix and the Carpet

118

A story that may have had some influence on E. Nesbit was Dickens's *Holiday Romance*. It is written in something like the Oswald style, though the humour is more adult-orientated than E. Nesbit's own sense of comedy. The children of *Holiday Romance*, confronted with the sadly unromantic realities of life as imposed on them by adults, resolve to 'throw our thoughts into something educational for the grown-up people, hinting to them how things ought to be'. The result is three stories supposedly written by the children. ('Romance. From the Pen of Miss Alice Rainbird (aged 7)' is in fact the well-known *Magic Fishbone*.) The introductory story often reminds one of Oswald trying out an elevated manner.

'On the beauteous faces of the Nymphs dejection sat enthroned. All four reclined under the willow for some minutes without speaking, till at length the bride of the colonel poutingly observed, "It's of no use pretending any more, and we had better give it up." '

Holiday Romance

The other writer one thinks of in connection with E. Nesbit is Kenneth Grahame. His *The Golden Age* and *Dream Days* were intended for adult readers; the point of likeness between him and E. Nesbit is in the imaginative games played by the children in their books. It would be hard to prove more than an affinity between the child characters of the two writers—so many children play such games, and, reading the books, must have found that they too shared that affinity. But Kenneth Grahame and E. Nesbit were certainly alike in remembering vividly what childhood felt like.

E. Nesbit does, in fact, make a complimentary reference to him in *The Phoenix and the Carpet*—the children's father brings home a 'ripping book from the library, called *The Golden Age*'. She quite often gives an opinion on contemporary writing for children in her own books. Oswald is particularly useful for the purpose. The Bastables' tastes in reading are extremely sound (and also perfectly credible as the opinions of real children). They range from whole-hearted admiration of Kipling, through a guarded judgment by Oswald on *The Daisy Chain* ('a first-rate book for girls and little boys'), to a definitely critical attitude towards the poorer types of children's books. Oswald breaks out into parody of 'the books they give you for a prize at a girls' school', but finds it too hard to keep up for long. Through him, E. Nesbit mocks gently at the *cliché* of the conventional story-book farm-house.

'If we had been in a story-book the miller's wife would have taken us into the neat sanded kitchen where the old oak settle was black with time and rubbing, and dusted chairs for us—old brown Windsor chairs—and given us each a glass of sweet-scented cowslip wine and a thick slice of rich home-made cake. And there would have been fresh roses in an old china bowl on the table. As it was, she asked us all into the parlour and gave us Eiffel Tower lemonade and Marie biscuits. The chairs in her parlour were "bent wood", and no flowers, except some wax ones under a glass shade.'

The Wouldbegoods

A piece of realistic observation which may still be a useful antidote to too much cowslip wine and old oak settle in a story.

She does some more mild bubble-pricking in *Five Children and It*, in a skit on those historical romances for the young which were not so accurately and conscientiously written then as they generally are now. Cyril, Anthea and

Jane have wished to be inside a besieged castle. Robert, trying to join them, meets the besieging army. It looks 'exactly like the pictures Robert had so often admired in the historical romances', and talks after the same fashion. The leader is splendidly armed:

'His shield was thirteenth century, while the sword was of the pattern used in the Peninsular War. The cuirass was of the time of Charles I, and the helmet dated from the Second Crusade. The arms on the shield were very grand—three red running lions on a blue ground. The tents were of the latest brand approved of by our modern War Office, and the whole appearance of camp, army and leader might have been a shock to some. . . .

"Where dwellest thou, young knave?" inquired the man with the largest steel cap.

"Over there," said Robert, and directly he had said it he knew he ought to have said "Yonder".'

Five Children and It

And there were the moral stories, a type of book that few children now have to read. But the progress from the overtly edifying pre-Victorian children's books to the more entertaining stories of today was not made all in one leap. There was plenty of solid edification to be found at the beginning of the century. The Bastables know and distrust moral stories. Daisy has read a lot; they have helped to make a white mouse of her.

'*Ministering Children*, and *Anna Ross, or The Orphan of Waterloo*, and *Ready Work for Willing Hands*, and *Elsie, or Like a Little Candle*, and even a horrid little blue book about the something or other of Little Sins.'

The Wouldbegoods

There were stories about pious children, children who did

good, children who were punished for worldly vanity. Oswald had read one of these:

'... where there was a girl called Theodosia, and she could play brilliant trebles on the piano in duets, but the other girl knew all about leeches which is much more useful and golden deedy.'

The Wouldbegoods

Children plied with this sort of literature must often have echoed Tony Lumpkin's cry of, 'If I'm to have any good, let it come of itself; not to keep dinging it, dinging it into one so.' But because E. Nesbit laughs at the moral stories, one may overlook the fact that there *is* quite a strand of moralising in her own books. In fact, a child probably will overlook it, because of the skill with which she wove it in. She knew it was no use trying to 'ding it in', that children hate anything which pretends it is going to amuse them and then shows itself in its true colours. E. Nesbit's own characters are thoroughly disgusted when the magic carpet tries to play this trick on them. In an access of Christmas-time virtue, the girls suggest asking it to take them 'somewhere we should have the chance to do some good and kind action. It would be an adventure just the same.' No one is at all pleased when the carpet stays put just where it is on the nursery floor.

'"Oh! I see what it means," said Robert, with deep disgust. "It's like the end of a fairy-story in a Sunday magazine. How perfectly beastly!"

"You mean it means we can do kind and good actions where we are? I see. I suppose it wants us to carry coals for the cook or make clothes for the bare heathens. Well, I simply won't. And the last day and everything. Look here!" Cyril spoke loudly and firmly. "We want to go somewhere really interesting, where we have a chance of doing something good and kind; we don't want to do it here, but somewhere else. See?" '

The Phoenix and the Carpet

Entertainment first, edification in passing—it would be an unnatural child who wanted the order reversed. That is what E. Nesbit provides. Sometimes she does a little moralising by the way. (Here, for instance, she actually *has* put forward the idea of doing kind actions at home, disarming criticism by making Cyril and Robert react just as her readers would have done.) She will put a few remarks on selfishness or thoughtlessness into the Bastable stories, arising from the situations the children get into, and usually made with engaging solemnity by Oswald himself. Or she weaves the moral into the plot. The magic of *The House of Arden* is conditional on good behaviour. Elfrida and Edred can find the room with the magic chests only when they have gone a day without quarrelling. In a way the whole of *Five Children and It* is a moral story, on the vanity of human wishes. First of all, beauty brings the children nothing but inconvenience. Next they wish,

'"... To be rich beyond the dreams of something or other."

"Avarice," said Jane.

"So it is," said the Fairy unexpectedly. "But it won't do you much good, that's one comfort," it muttered to itself.'

Five Children and It

Nor does it. The children have a whole pit full of unexchangeable spade guineas on their hands, and only the timely sunset dissolves the magic and saves them from trouble with the police. The moral is embedded in a very funny story.

E. Nesbit did not make her books a pulpit, either for

obtrusive moralising in general or for personal views of her own—one can read them all without getting much idea of the author as a person. But in the *Girl's Own Paper* articles she tells what use she did make of her own childhood experiences. There was the exploration of the Nile, and another incident that she also used in *The Wouldbegoods*.

'Is it possible that I have forgotten the dreadful day when my brother Alfred shot a fox?

He drew me mysteriously aside one morning after breakfast.

"Daisy," he said, "can you keep a secret?"

I could, I asseverated.

He drew me into his room, locked the door, and then opening a cupboard displayed the body of a big dog-fox.

"Where did you get it?"

"I shot it."

"Oh, poor thing."

"Poor thing indeed," repeated my brother indignantly. "Don't you know no one would ever speak to me again if they knew I had shot a fox?"

"Then why did you?" was the natural rejoinder.

"I didn't mean to. I was out this morning after wood-pigeons, and I saw something move in the bushes. I thought it was a rabbit and I fired, and it was *this*. What shall I do with it?"

"Bury it, we can have a splendid funeral," I said.

"You baby!"

I was constantly forgetting that Alfred, at seventeen, was grown-up, and that our old games no longer interested him.

"Well, stuff it, then."

. . . But we never stuffed it. We never even succeeded in curing the skin, which after a while cried aloud for vengeance so unmistakably that we had to take it out and bury it secretly.'

The Bastables discover their fox already shot (accident-
ally, by Denny, who was trying to release it from a trap),
but are not too old to enjoy a funeral complete with Noel's
Burial Ode.

Then there was a tower that the Nesbits passed on their
travels in France, which caught Edith's imagination.

'On the way we passed a large yellow-stone castle on a
hill. Most of the castle was in ruins, but a great square
tower, without door or window, still stood as strong and
firm as on the day when the last stone was pattted into place
with the trowel. We wandered round this tower in vain,
trying to find a door.

"But it is that there is no door," said our driver at last;
"within that tower is buried a treasure. . . ."

We drove on; presently we stopped at a little wayside
shrine, with a painted image of St John in it, and a little
shell of holy water. At the side of that shrine was a stone
with an iron ring in it. Nothing more was needed to convince
me that this was the entrance to a subterranean passage,
leading to the tower where the treasure was. Imagine the
dreams that occupied me for the rest of the drive!'

In *The Phoenix and the Carpet*, years later, she made the
dreams come true for Cyril, Robert, Anthea and Jane—
subterranean passage, treasure, trap-door and all. They
emerge at the identical shrine on their way to restore the
treasure to its rightful owner.

Right at the end of her life, E. Nesbit recalled another
of her childhood experiences, and made use of it in *Five
of Us—And Madeline*.

She had been bored staying in a doctor's household in
London.

'One night I went into the surgery and found the bottles
of medicine which his assistant had made up, standing in a

row waiting for their white paper wrappers. I didn't in the least realise what I was doing when I thought to escape from my boredom by mixing the contents of these bottles in a large jug, and then in partially filling up the bottles again with the mixture. When I had filled and corked them all, I slipped away; it was done in pure mischief, with no thought of consequences; but when I woke that night in bed and suddenly remembered that I had heard that medicines that were given for some complaints were bad for others, and absolutely harmful, my heart stood still. Suppose some poor sick person died, whom Dr —— would have cured, because I had mixed his medicine with something else. I fully resolved to own up the next morning, but the next morning I reflected that perhaps some of the people that had taken my mixture might die of it, and then I should be hanged for murder; it seemed to me wiser to wait and see what happened. If anyone did die, and Dr —— were accused of poisoning his patients, I would come forward in the court of justice, as people did in the books, and own that I, and I alone, had been to blame, making my confession among the sympathetic tears of usher and jury, the judge himself not remaining dry-eyed. This scene so much appealed to me that I almost forgot that before it could be enacted somebody would have to die of my mixture.'

Madeline, staying with a doctor uncle, is bored too, and tells the same story to Clifford and Martin, who have been out on their own without taking her.

'"When I couldn't think of anything to do for ages and ages I went into the dispensary. You know where they put all the different bottles of medicine for ill people. Only no corks . . . I wanted to mix them all up. And I mixed all the things in the different bottles".'

Five of Us—And Madeline

But E. Nesbit gives the story another twist, making it a

rather pathetic ruse of Madeline's to frighten her cousins and make them feel sorry for neglecting her.

' "I never did," said Madeline, who was in bed; "I said I had mixed up what was in the bottles on the bench. There were only two. They were soaking. They were just being washed out. Now then!"

"But you know we thought . . ."

"Why did you want us to believe . . . ?" said our hero and his brother together.

"To pay you out for leaving me alone," said Madeline. "You always say I never think of anything, and that I'm a white rabbit or a mouse. But you see I can think of things, only I don't always do what I think of. And I don't care *what* you do to me. So there!" '

Five of Us—And Madeline

E. Nesbit might use this kind of memory in her stories— but there is no trace of the nerve-racking terrors of her imagination. If the children in her books get into a frightening situation, at any rate it is not a private nightmare. Even in the much-criticised episode of the Ugly-Wuglies, in *The Enchanted Castle*, Gerald and Mabel face the uncanny creatures together. She selected skilfully, leaving aside her distressing personal memories, picking on details that would strike a cheerful answering note in her readers.

She avoided, too, any temptation that may have confronted her to put forward political views in her stories. There were plenty of sentimental stories about poor children, and if E. Nesbit had merely added to their number, she would probably not be read today. It is when she has to deal with poverty, in *The Railway Children*, without the saving grace of Bastable humour, that she most often lapses into sentimentality. But there are only a few occasions, exceptions that prove the rule, when she does take advantage of her readers and let any of her feelings on controversial subjects of the day into her stories. Dickie Harding, living happily in the past, attacks the present which he knows from the slum child's point of view; in *The Story of the Amulet*, Cyril and the rest travel into the future and find it a Utopian paradise according to the early Socialists. The chapter dates now, but in that most varied and exciting of E. Nesbit's fantasies it is not a very large stumbling-block.

Even if E. Nesbit had chosen to write about the poor children of Deptford for whom she organised parties, she would inevitably have described them from the outside, without the same realism she could employ in the Bastable stories. As it was, with the sole exception of Dickie Harding —who anyway turns out to be a nobleman by birth—she took for her characters the kind of children she thoroughly knew and understood from the inside. That is what one notices first and remembers longest—the sheer reality of the children in her books. They talk, quarrel and play exactly as children do talk, quarrel and play; as E. Nesbit did herself with Alfred and Henry. Realistic conversation is one of her strongest points.

' "Let's go to Kew in the meantime."

"I'd rather go in a steamer," said Robert, and the girls laughed.

"That's right," said Cyril, "*be* funny. I would."

"Well, he was, rather," said Anthea.

"I wouldn't think, Squirrel, if it hurts you so," said Robert kindly.

"Oh, shut up," said Cyril, "or else talk about Kew." '

The Story of the Amulet

There is a strong similarity between all the Nesbit children. They are all given to scoring off each other in this way. They are enterprising; they love adventure and romance. At the same time they are to some degree realists. In a large family, brothers and sisters do not scruple to say plainly when someone is making a fool of himself, so there is bound to be a certain amount of common-sense about. They are all remarkably free from adult interference —not because their parents neglect them, but because E. Nesbit found it more convenient to get parents out of the way. (The best-remembered adult in any of her stories is not a parent at all, but Albert's good-natured uncle.) They hate the very thought of being bored, and if they feel boredom approaching, have plenty of ideas to ward it off. They all invent their own games, and are never happier than when playing at *The Jungle Book*, 'reproducing the attitudes of statues seen either in the British Museum, or in Father's big photograph book', or even playing all alone, like Mabel in *The Enchanted Castle*, who is discovered by the others dressed up in pink silk pretending to be an enchanted princess. How many children must have tried to work their own spells, like Caroline, Charlotte and Charles in *The Wonderful Garden*, or dressed up for the kind of acting game which occurs in *The Magic World* when the children are acting their own version of Rudel and the Lady of Tripoli, the girl, Alison, very much in charge of proceedings:

'"What ho! Ashore there!" shouted the captain.

"What ho!" said a voice from the shore, which, Alison explained, was disguised.

"We be three poor mariners," said Conrad by a happy effort of memory, "just newly come to shore. We seek news of the Princess of Tripoli."

"She's in her palace," said the disguised voice, "wait a minute and I'll tell her you're here. But what do you want her for? ('A poor minstrel of France' go on, Con.)"

"A poor minstrel of France," said Conrad, "(all right,

I remember) who has heard of the Princess's beauty, has come to lay, to lay—"

"His heart," said Alison.

"All right, I know. His heart at her something or other feet."

"Pretty feet," said Alison . . .

"Do shut up," said the Princess, stamping her foot. "Now then, Ken, go ahead. Ken, you say, 'Oh lady, I faint with rapture!' "

"I faint with rapture," said Kenneth stolidly. "Now I land, don't I?"

He landed and stared at the jewelled hand the Princess held out.

"At last, at last," she said, "but you ought to say that, Ken." '

Kenneth and the Carp (*The Magic World*)

Not so spontaneous as the Bastables' games, perhaps, but anyone who has ever been coerced into playing this kind of thing by a determined elder sister will at once recognise the ring of truth here.

Besides this family likeness, each Nesbit child also has a definite character of its own. And this means that in all the books, including the magic stories, the children themselves are as interesting as anything that happens to them, however startling. E. Nesbit herself really put her secret in a nutshell, describing one of her families to her readers, when she wrote,

'They were not particularly handsome, nor were they extra clever, nor extraordinarily good. But they were not bad sorts on the whole; in fact, they were rather like you.'

The Phoenix and the Carpet

v. The Books

In the Bastable family, who appear in *The Treasure Seekers*, E. Nesbit's first important creation, she immediately showed her powers of drawing lifelike children. They are absolutely convincing both as a family unit and as individuals—the conscientious Dora, Dicky the practical one, Noel the poet, Alice who was 'almost worthy to be a boy for some things', H.O. the youngest, and Oswald himself. E. Nesbit's boys are all well-drawn, and she managed to get right inside Oswald's skin. He tells the three Bastable stories, *The Story of the Treasure Seekers*, *The Wouldbegoods*, and *New Treasure Seekers*, in a precariously maintained third person, giving himself away with remarks about 'Oswald . . . who was, I think, gifted by fate with the far-seeingness of a born general'. All the stories are coloured by his outlook, from the moment when he opens with his opinions on how to begin a story.

'I have read books myself, and I know how beastly it is when a story begins, "Alas!" said Hildegarde with a deep sigh, "we must look our last on this ancestral home"—and then someone else says something—and you don't know for pages and pages where the home is, or who Hildegarde is, or anything about it.'

The Story of the Treasure Seekers

Oswald has a true brotherly contempt for girls, especially poor Dora; he and Dickie view the Wouldbegood Society with deep suspicion. His style carries E. Nesbit over what might otherwise have been some sticky moments. The reconciliation with the rich Indian uncle, for instance, might easily have made uncomfortably sentimental reading, but seen through Oswald's eyes it is a thoroughly satisfactory happy ending, with a touch of fairy-tale about the sudden abundance of presents and good food. In fact, E. Nesbit was never to do this kind of thing quite so successfully again.

The chapters of the Bastable books are all more or less self-contained incidents, because of the serial form in which they first appeared (not in the same order as in the books). Each chapter of *The Treasure Seekers* is a variation on the original idea of fortune-hunting. The Wouldbegood Society of the next book does not occupy the children's attention quite so exclusively, but it was another productive idea. E. Nesbit's comic invention also has full play in these three books. She describes each incident step by step, rising to its climax in a comic crescendo. One of the best is the episode of the improvised circus, ending in the hilarious chase of the 'black (and destined to be Learned) pig'. Oswald's commentary further enlivens matters. E. Nesbit gives a delightful picture of Oswald trying to keep his hat on by will-power when he and Alice—heavily disguised as Miss Daisy Dolman and the Right Honourable Miss Etheltruda Bustler—visit an editor's office.

'The author cannot deny that now Oswald wished he hadn't. The elastic was moving slowly, but too surely. Oswald tried to check its career by swelling out the bump on the back of his head, but he could not think of the right way to do this.'

New Treasure Seekers

The Railway Children was the next book E. Nesbit wrote about children in everyday life—if, that is, it can be called everyday life. It is arguable that a series of incidents such as rescuing trains, rescuing wounded boys, rescuing babies from fires and rescuing foreign refugees constitute just as much of a fantasy as marvellous adventures on a flying carpet. The story cried out for the liveliness of the Bastables, and the pen of Oswald, to redeem it from sentimentality. One longs for a breath of Bastable fresh air, in which just one of the rescues would turn out to be superfluous. The whole thing is just a bit too close to the average well-meaning children's story of the period. The children themselves have many good moments—even so, there is not quite the convincing family feeling that exists between the children in most of E. Nesbit's books. She concentrates on the eldest, Roberta, who thinks a great deal about her mother. A full-scale relationship between adult and child was a new departure for E. Nesbit, and not one that suited her powers very well. There is far too much dwelling on Mother's bravery, and indeed everyone else's bravery too. Mother has to write to make ends meet; obviously this touch originated in the struggles of E. Nesbit's early married life, and she must have partly identified herself with Mother of *The Railway Children*. Perhaps this one lapse from the habit of objectivity which served her so well helps to account for the difference in quality of this story. Or perhaps, aiming at an effect of pathos more popular then than now in children's books—one thinks of the sufferings of Frances Hodgson Burnett's Sara Crewe, like the Railway Children suddenly plunged into poverty—E. Nesbit had not seen clearly that her own talents lay in a more cheerful direction.

Opinions differ about *The Railway Children*; some rank it among the best of E. Nesbit's work, and it has been successfully broadcast and televised. My own view is that it is not in the same class as the rest of her books, and without them might not have survived to the television age at all —and that a discriminating child will recognise the difference in quality subconsciously, enjoying *The Railway Children*, but not with the same satisfying kind of enjoyment as the Bastable books provide.

E. Nesbit's next book about 'everyday life', *The Wonderful Garden*, does not quite fit into that category. It borders on fantasy; there is *almost* magic in it, but not quite. It might have been especially written for children who feel wistfully that 'things happen to children in books', and magic must be aggravatingly easy to find, if only one knew where to look. (In fact, E. Nesbit begins with a shrewd little advertisement for herself; Caroline, Charlotte and Charles have been reading *The Story of the Amulet*, and it is that book that turns their thoughts to magic.) The children's half-hopeful, half-doubtful attitude is beautifully observed. Although the spells never quite work, E. Nesbit does not disillusion them. The appearance of a long-dead ancestress has its rational explanation, but the Wonderful Garden itself remains a mysterious place, and E. Nesbit lets an elusive magic feeling linger about the star-like flowers grown from the seeds of Heart's Desire. This is the gentlest of all her books. For the second time she lets girls predominate over boys in the family—the only other occasion when she does this is in *The Railway Children*; Charles is a little subdued by mere force of numbers. *The Wonderful Garden* is not so lively as either the Bastable books or the earlier fantasies, but it has a charm of its own.

Then, right at the end of her life, E. Nesbit returned to the Bastable manner in *Five of Us—And Madeline*. The situation is the same—family fortunes lost at first, parents conveniently absent, the children living in Aunt Emma's house with 'a sort of relation called Miss Knox'. Aunt Emma's house is 'small and new and mimsey', but Clifford philosophically compares their lot with the fate of children in books.

'Sometimes when boys' fathers lose their money they have to go and live in wretched sunless slums with absolutely indignant relatives, I believe, and beg for their bread till someone adopts them, and the book ends with ponies and cricket-bats and a high rate of pocket money almost dream-like.'

Five of Us—And Madeline

This might be Oswald talking, and Clifford is a character created on much the same lines. He tells the story in the same mixture of first and third person, and holds similar opinions on authorship.

'An author with a muddly mind is an awful thing. I know some like this, and you can never tell what they are driving at until you have finished the story, and not always then.'

Five of Us—And Madeline

If the children are not so clear individually as the Bastables, there is the same family atmosphere. E. Nesbit had not forgotten how to convey that; and even in her old age, she could describe the joy of finding and appropriating an empty cottage in a wood, remembering exactly what it felt like to be one of the young explorers 'with grim boots and undaunted hearts'. But the book is not precisely a repetition of the Bastables. There is an innovation—Madeline herself, the only alien among E. Nesbit's children. She does not quite belong, she sniffs, she is sometimes spiteful because she is unhappy at being left out. She is, as it were, an extension of E. Nesbit's sympathy to those children who are not lucky enough to belong to a large, cheerful family.

While still writing stories about the Bastables, E. Nesbit had launched out into her fantasies, in *Five Children and It* and its sequels, *The Phoenix and the Carpet* and *The Story of the Amulet*. Part of the secret of her success in this vein

is that the human children who are the central figures—and
with whom the child reader will identify itself—are themselves as lively as the children in the everyday-life books.
She does not let her powers of fantastic invention run away
with her at their expense. Cyril, Robert and their sisters have
not, of course, so much scope simply to be themselves as
the Bastables had, because strange adventures take up a
good deal of their time. But they are far from being mere
pegs for the author's imaginings. Through all their adventures they remain their individual selves, and—like the
Bastables—an unmistakable family unit. One of their
characteristics is a liking for argument and a gift for repartee
—friendly rudeness of the kind that becomes a point of
honour. It does not desert them even when they are in an
underground passage, expecting any moment to come
across 'dungeons, and chains, and knobbly bare bones',
as Robert ghoulishly prophesies.

'"I wish you hadn't put bones into your heads," said
Jane as they went along.

"I didn't; you always had them. More bones than brains,"
said Robert.'

The Phoenix and the Carpet

Fortunately they are level-headed children, for the magic
creatures and their powers get them into all kinds of awkward situations, and they have to spend a lot of time trying
to explain the incredible and pacify people. They hardly
ever have a chance to be mere passive onlookers of the
magic.

These magic creatures were among E. Nesbit's most
brilliant and original ideas. 'Before Anthea and Cyril and
the others had been a week in the country they had found a
fairy', she writes at the beginning of *Five Children and It*.
But her fairy was not one of the 'painty-winged, wand-

waving, sugar-and-shake-your-head, company' anathema-
tised by Kipling's Puck. Nor did she try her hand at the
true fairies of tradition, the uncanny and malicious Good
People. Her real gift was not for poetic fantasy but for the
comic spirit in which she imagined the endearing, bad-
tempered, slightly grotesque Psammead (pronounced 'Sam-
myad'). We have E. Nesbit's own word for it that H. R.
Millar's familiar illustrations to the Psammead stories give a
very faithful idea of the creature as she saw it—brown,
furry, with bat's ears and eyes which it shoots in and out
like telescopes. It is hardly surprising that the children do
not recognise it for a fairy at once.

'"What on earth is it?" said Jane. "Shall we take it
home?"

The thing turned its long eyes to look at her, and said—

"Does she always talk nonsense, or is it only the rubbish
on her head that makes her silly?"

It looked scornfully at Jane's hat as it spoke.'

Five Children and It

In this vein the Psammead continues, commenting acidly
on the children's appearance and behaviour and the
stupidity of their wishes. However, it is really an affectionate
creature, and after being rescued at the beginning of *The
Story of the Amulet*, starts the children off on their adventures in that book by showing them where to buy the
amulet—characteristically pointing out, all the same, 'I
haven't *got* to do this for you, it's just my own generous
kindness that makes me tell you about it'. Its astringent
manner and bad-tempered remarks make it most entertaining company; in fact, the Psammead is a very definite
person, unlike most fictional fairies.

The same can be said of the Phoenix, that courteous,
elegant and conceited bird. It sets great store by proper

form and ceremony, and is delighted when Robert in-
advertently sums up the whole of its Greek ode of invocation in one English hexameter. In spite of its newly acquired
Cockney, it has rather less grasp of modern life than the
Psammead. It gives E. Nesbit plenty of opportunities to
make magic collide with real life, and this opposition of the
familiar and the fantastic was the particular *forte* of her
imagination. She establishes the point of meeting, with an
eye always open for a comic situation, and then describes the
results. In these first three fantasies particularly, she
exploits the humorous possibilities of inter-weaving magic
and daily life—the Psammead's wishes that never turn out
as the children expect, the visit of the Phoenix to the fire
insurance office bearing its name to demand a ceremony of
worship, the cook and burglar who are transported to a
South Sea island by carpet, and the half clergyman brought
to marry them (half only, because he stands partly on
magic carpet, partly on a darned patch), the Babylonian
Queen in London bringing her jewellery out of the British
Museum by magic, or wishing the City men were dressed
like the Babylonians of her court:

'The moment the almost fainting Psammead had blown
itself out every man in Throgmorton Street appeared
abruptly in Babylonian full dress. . . .

A stupefied silence fell on them.

"I say," a youth who had always been fair-haired broke
that silence, "it's only fancy of course—something wrong
with my eyes—but you chaps do look so rum."

"Rum!" said his friend. "Look at *you*. You in a sash!
My hat! And your hair's gone black and you've got a beard.
It's my belief we've been poisoned." '

The Story of the Amulet

The Story of the Amulet is perhaps the best of all E.

Nesbit's magic stories. It combines the conversation of the children with the comments of the Psammead, and the contrast between depressing London lodgings and colourful magic adventures. It also has a much stronger narrative thread than is usual with E. Nesbit to join the episodes together. The children's search for the lost half of the amulet becomes exciting as well as amusing, especially when they discover that the priest Rekh-mara is after it too. And the vivid glimpses of ancient history fully repaid E. Nesbit's trouble over them—for in this story she had, for the first time, picked on a plot which needed research into its background (into several backgrounds, in fact). One of E. Nesbit's friends at this time was Dr Wallis Budge, Keeper of Egyptian and Assyrian Antiquities at the British Museum, to whom the book is dedicated. With his help, E. Nesbit did research into the backgrounds she needed—a prehistorical Egyptian village, Babylon, Tyre, Egypt again at the time of the Pharaohs, Atlantis.

Also in *The Story of the Amulet*, E. Nesbit introduces for the first time a touch of mystery and remoteness in her magic. The amulet itself has a kind of presiding spirit, which speaks to the children.

'Instantly the whole light of the world seemed to go out. The room was dark. The world outside was dark—darker than the darkest night that ever was. And all the sounds went out too, so that there was a silence deeper than any silence you have ever dreamed of imagining. . . . A faint, beautiful light began to show in the middle of the circle, and at the same moment a faint, beautiful voice began to speak. . . . And the voice grew, not so much in loudness as in sweetness (though it grew louder, too), till it was so sweet that you wanted to cry with pleasure just at the sound of it. It was like nightingales, and the sea . . .'

The children themselves at once see that:

'This was not like the things that had happened in the country when the Psammead gave them their wishes. That had been funny somehow, and this was not.'

The Story of the Amulet

And in this story E. Nesbit judged the right proportion of this new, remote magic to her more familiar 'funny' magic. Both the Psammead and the Amulet gain by being balanced one against the other.

She developed this new note further in *The Enchanted Castle*. Here too it begins by being balanced against the humorous side of the magic, but gradually she lets the weight swing right over to the poetically fantastic side. This happens partly because there is no magic creature with a character of its own like the Psammead or the Phoenix in the book. The ring of *The Enchanted Castle* has its own logic (involving a curious series of halved time sequences) but it is not nearly so cut and dried as the rules of the flying carpet or the Psammead's wishes, and there is no Psammead or Phoenix to guide and comment. The book gets off to an excellent start, when Gerald, Jimmy and Kathleen are kept wondering whether Mabel is 'pretending' or whether they really have wandered into magic—until the ring actually does make Mabel invisible, much to her own surprise. After that the children have to find out for themselves just how the magic works. While they are doing this, magic and real life coincide as they did in the earlier fantasies—the maidservant steals the ring, for instance, and to the bewilderment of herself and her young man finds that she is invisible, 'the biter bitten'. But once it is clear just what the ring does do, E. Nesbit shifts the emphasis to the enchanted atmosphere of the castle itself. The magic comes thick and fast. There are stone beasts that come alive, statues of gods that banquet by night with the children, an enchanted hall which is the heart of all the magic. The story rises to an almost mystical climax by moonlight.

'The moonbeam slants more and more; now it touches the far end of the stone, now it draws nearer and nearer to the middle of it, now at last it touches the very heart and centre of that central stone. And then it is as though a spring were touched, a fountain of light released. . . . Space is not; every place that one has seen or dreamed of is here. Time is not; into this instant is crowded all that one has ever done or dreamed of doing. It is a moment, and it is eternity.'

The Enchanted Castle

It is difficult not to feel that E. Nesbit's magic sometimes gets a little out of hand in *The Enchanted Castle*, rather more poetical and mysterious than she could comfortably manage. Not that this purely fantastic magic without the humours of the Psammead is not good of its kind—but one must make the reservation that other writers have done as well and better in that field, and E. Nesbit's real excellence lay in the other direction.

However, even if E. Nesbit's magic does occasionally get out of control in *The Enchanted Castle*, and it thus comes slightly below the standard of its three predecessors, it does not come very far below them. One criticism has often been levelled against it—mistakenly, I think—that the episode of the Ugly-Wuglies is horrific. The Ugly-Wuglies are creatures constructed out of broom-sticks, umbrellas, coats and paper masks, which come alive by the magic of the ring. Having no roofs to their mouths, they speak without consonants. Gerald and Mabel try to keep them in the castle. At the last moment they become suspicious.

'There were screams from ladies' voices, the hoarse, determined shouts of strong Ugly-Wuglies roused to resistance, and, worse than all, the steady pushing open of that narrow stone door that had almost closed upon the ghastly crew. Through the chink of it they could be seen, a writhing black crowd against the light of the bicycle lamp; a padded hand reached round the door; stick-boned arms stretched out angrily.... And the tone of their consonantless speech was no longer conciliatory and ordinary; it was threatening, full of the menace of unbearable horrors.'

The Enchanted Castle

Certainly this is a less genial grotesquerie than that of the Psammead. But is it in fact frightening? Most children love a few bogies in their stories, and if deprived of them are quite likely to invent their own. The things that really frighten them are apt to lie deeper than any such description of horrors from the outside, in private, unexpected corners of the mind. To take examples from E. Nesbit's own experience—who on earth could have expected that the words *Débit de Tabac* would remind a child of her father's grave? Yet the same child treasured a chicken-bone, hoping it was human, and arriving at an inn, 'just the place where travellers are always murdered in Christmas stories', remarks that her teeth 'chattered with terror, but there was a certain pleasure in the excitement all the same'. For most children, the Ugly-Wuglies surely come into the category of pleasurable story-book terrors. For one thing, E. Nesbit is extremely explicit about them—that full-blooded phrase, 'the ghastly crew', indicates their real story-book bogy nature—the really frightening is the half-revealed, the unexplained. One other moment in E. Nesbit's writings would, if she had done more than dwell on it very lightly and briefly, have been more likely to frighten an imaginative child. This is the prototype of *The Magic City*, a short story called *The Town In The Library In The Town In The Library*, when two children building a toy town find themselves inside it, find their house and another town built on the library floor—in that town their house again—a glimpse of mirror-nightmare beside which the Ugly-Wuglies look quite comfortable creatures.

The House of Arden and *Harding's Luck* stand together because of their very closely connected plots. Strictly speaking, they have only one plot between them; while she was still writing *The House of Arden*, E. Nesbit prepared the way for its sequel. Not perhaps from the beginning—when Edred and Elfrida first meet Dickie in the time of James I, he shows them a bill with an address from their own time on it. It is a more well-to-do address than she gives Dickie in his own book, and when she explains it there, it has the feel of something explained *away*. Perhaps she first introduced Dickie to redress the balance a little on the boys' side of things—Elfrida is older than Edred, a more admirable character, and generally tends to steal the limelight. But towards the end of *The House of Arden* E. Nesbit begins to prepare the ground with the story of the lost branch of the family.

Besides being so closely connected with each other, the two books stand rather apart from the rest of E. Nesbit's stories. The plot is on much more melodramatic lines than usual. Lost heirs, kidnappings, an *Oliver Twist*-like incident when Dickie is made to be a burglar's accomplice—these do not occur seriously in E. Nesbit's other books. The melodramatic touches are neatly done; even the necessary 'strawberry mark', in this case an old-fashioned baby's rattle, is cleverly worked into the story. Dickie himself is partly responsible for this difference in tone from the other fantasies. As a slum child who is the rightful Lord Arden, he is a fictional child rather than a startlingly real one like the middle-class children of E. Nesbit's other books. In this new vein Dickie, rather surprisingly, does come off. Perilously as she sometimes approaches mawkishness with his physical handicap (a lame leg), E. Nesbit manages to steer clear of it most of the time. In particular, she presents his life on the open road with the tramp Beale with much imaginative sympathy.

The missing-heir theme belongs to the present, and E. Nesbit saves most of it for *Harding's Luck*. The magic excursions into the past belong mostly to *The House of Arden*. In this book E. Nesbit began to invent another magic creature. The rustic Mouldiwarp is a lesser edition of the Psammead, crossly obliged to help the children, sharp-tongued, but with its heart in the right place.

'"I've *got* to let you find me again. Don't upset yourself," it said bitterly.'

The House of Arden

This is the familiar grudging attitude, and on its first appearance, the Mouldiwarp really promises very well to follow in the Sand-fairy's footsteps. But once it has shown the way to get back into the past, it fades out of the picture. There is no need for the children to see it at the beginning of each chapter, and the magic becomes more like the magic in *The Enchanted Castle* than in *Five Children and It*. Nor does the creature get many chances in *Harding's Luck*, where Dickie has his own way to go into the past. But it does turn out in that book to have a comparative and superlative, the Mouldierwarp and the Mouldiestwarp—rather perfunctory creatures who appear in a scene which is not one of E. Nesbit's best.

Although one must regret a little the lost possibilities of the Mouldiwarp, the pure magic of *The House of Arden* is very good indeed. Its scope is less ambitious than in *The Enchanted Castle*, and her powers in this direction show here at their best. The historical scenes themselves are nothing like as convincing as the historical scenes of *The Story of the Amulet*, and do not read as if E. Nesbit really meant them to be for the style is near to the 'romantic' vein she parodies in *Five Children and It*. They really read more like a lively series of charades than anything else—the magic involves dressing up in clothes of the appropriate period, which adds to this feeling. But the magical transitions to these scenes are the best thing in the book. Others besides the children move about in time; there is an old nurse who keeps reappearing and knows magic herself. The interweaving of past and present, over and beyond the children's own journeys, keeps a current of mystery and magic flowing, a sense that Edred and Elfrida are meeting with larger things than just bits of time neatly boxed into chapters. Like all good magic, the enchantment has its rules; the children break them when they try to open a chest and find clothes of another time than the ones laid ready for them, and discover that 'he that will not when he may, shall have not when he will'. The sense of magic in the elusive attic room where the chests are stored, the cooing voices of doves that makes time an illusion, are all delightful products of E. Nesbit's imagination. One scarcely minds that in all this magic the object of the journeys—to find the Arden treasure—is often forgotten, and dealt with at the end of *Harding's Luck* only as part of a general clearing-up process.

Not much need be said of *The Magic City*—although had anyone but E. Nesbit written it, it would show much better than it does when measured against the standard of her other books. For once, she had an excellent idea and never rose to it; she develops it in a rather prosaic, plodding manner foreign to the other fantasies. Philip, the hero, also lacks the appeal of the children belonging to E. Nesbit's large families. He has no brothers and sisters to argue with, and only gradually makes friends with Lucy. But when, in *Wet Magic*, she returns to a family of children, she shows that she had not lost her touch. Especially in the early chapters, before the magic sets in, the children are as lively and lifelike as ever—in particular Bernard, who 'took a melancholy pride in being the kind of boy who always gets caught'. The imperious and bad-tempered Mermaid rescued by the children at first looks almost as though she will be a companion for the Psammead, the Phoenix and the Mouldiwarp. She is summoned to the top of her tank by the recitation of 'Sabrina Fair'.

'There was a heaving and stirring of the seaweed and fish tail, something gleamed white, through the brown something white parted the seaweed, two white hands parted it, and a face came to the surface of the rather dirty water and—there was no doubt about it—spoke.

"Translucent wave, indeed!" was what the face said. "I wonder you're not ashamed to speak the invocation over a miserable cistern like this. What do you want?"'

Wet Magic

Unfortunately salt water sweetens her temper when she gets back to the sea. But children enjoyed, and still do enjoy, both these lesser Nesbit stories. Noël Coward in his autobiography tells how he used to buy back numbers of the *Strand Magazine* in order to read E. Nesbit's stories, including *The Magic City*.

'I hoarded my pocket money until I could buy a whole

year's worth in order to read the E. Nesbit story right through without having to wait for the next instalment. I read *The Phoenix and the Carpet*, and *Five Children and It*, also *The Magic City*, but there were a few numbers missing from that year, so I stole a coral necklace from a visiting friend of Mother's, pawned it for five shillings, and bought the complete book at the Army and Navy Stores. . . . In later years I told E. Nesbit of this little incident and I regret to say she was delighted.'

VI. Conclusion

E. Nesbit won an immediate success with her children's books. It has proved to be lasting. Today she is read by children who lead lives very different from those of the characters in her books and their original readers. Besides being published in England and the United States, she has been translated and published in Holland, the Scandinavian countries, Poland, Germany and Israel. In dramatised form, several of her books have been popular as radio serial plays. She has had considerable influence on other children's authors. Writers as different as Noël Coward and C. S. Lewis remember the pleasure they had in reading her books as children. C. S. Lewis, writing about his childhood, recalls,

'Much better than either of these [*Sir Nigel* and *A Yankee at the Court of King Arthur*] was E. Nesbit's trilogy, *Five Children and It*, *The Phoenix and the Wishing Carpet*, and *The Amulet*. The last did most for me. It first opened my eyes to antiquity, the "dark backward and abysm of time". I can still re-read it with delight.'

It is now over sixty years since E. Nesbit wrote *The Treasure Seekers*, and she is still as popular as ever—proof that she was writing for and about the essential child of any time, not just the Edwardian child whose parents took the *Pall Mall* or the *Strand Magazine*. In fact there is extraordinarily little anywhere in her stories to remind the child reader of today that the children in the books are not his exact contemporaries—an occasional remark about clothes, Oswald's observations on the usefulness of girl's petticoats or the Psammead's question about the hat Jane wore to go digging in a gravel-pit on her summer holiday, the fact that when the Bastables and the family of *Five of Us—And Madeline* become poor they are taken away from school. But these are the merest externals. Even the old-fashioned children's names are beginning to come back into favour. E. Nesbit's great gift was to remember just what it felt like to be a child—witness her vivid reminiscences, written when she was in her late thirties—to know exactly what would amuse and entertain a child, and to be able to put it down on paper. She did not write above her readers' heads, but nor did she write down to them. Oswald Bastable, for instance, often suggests the use of a dictionary; she was not afraid of introducing children to new words. On the other hand, she does not often indulge in jokes aimed only at adult readers.

Indeed, she seldom went to any extremes in her children's books. The children in them are real—neither improbably virtuous or wicked, as Victorian story-book children sometimes were, nor improbably clever and intrepid, as the tendency is today. She had of course limitations; her poetic imagination was much more limited than her comic imagination. But at her best her limitations are quite set off by her other qualities. She had at her command two great steadying influences; realism and humour. They leaven the most fantastic adventures in her books—and the conversation and homely adventures of the children who do *not* have the luck to meet with magic rings or carpets, Sand-fairies or Phoenixes, are just as entertaining as the travels of those who do. After amusing children for sixty years, there is every reason to think that E. Nesbit's books will go on amusing new generations of children for another sixty years or more.

VII. Summaries of plots

The following are brief summaries of the plots of E. Nesbit's principal children's stories, with the date of first publication in book form.

I. STORIES OF EVERYDAY LIFE

The Story of the Treasure Seekers 1899

The chief characters are the Bastables—Oswald, Dora, Dickie, Alice, Noel and H. O. Albert-next-door and his amiable uncle also appear. The Bastables try to restore the family fortunes from their 'poor but honest circs in a semi-detached house in the Lewisham Road'. Each child suggests a method of fortune-restoring. The rich and benevolent Indian uncle provides a happy ending.

The Wouldbegoods 1901

Now living in 'an affluent mansion on Blackheath', the Bastables get up to mischief and are sent to stay in the country under the care of Albert's uncle. They are joined by Denny and Daisy, the two 'white mice'—though Denny at least becomes less mouse-like under Bastable influence. Daisy and Dora persuade the rest to form 'a society for being good', which leads them into many misadventures.

New Treasure Seekers 1904

Further exploits of the Bastables, both before and after the restoration of the family fortunes.

The Railway Children 1906

Father is unjustly sent to prison; Roberta (Bobby), Peter, Phyllis and their mother are reduced to poverty and go to live in the country. The children are fascinated by the railway and have adventures connected with it. All comes right in the end, through the offices of a benevolent old gentleman who befriends the children.

The Wonderful Garden 1911

Caroline, Charlotte and Charles go to stay with their anthropologist great-uncle. They hide Rupert, who is running away from his schoolmaster, and try to work their own magic. Finding the seeds of Heart's Desire, they plant them in the Wonderful Garden. When they give their uncle his desire—two old books of charms they have discovered—they get theirs, to go and see their parents in India.

Five of Us—And Madeline 1925

Clifford, Alan, Olive, Martin and Carlotta are a lively family on Bastable lines, with the addition of 'the fell Madeline', a cousin who does not quite fit in and yet longs to be accepted as one of them.

2. STORIES OF MAGIC

Five Children and It 1902

Cyril, Robert, Anthea, Jane and their baby brother, the Lamb, go to stay in the country. They find It, the Psammead or Sand-fairy, which grants them a wish a day.

The Phoenix and the Carpet 1904

The same family have adventures with a Phoenix and a flying carpet during their winter holidays.

The Story of the Amulet 1906

Cyril and the rest rescue the Psammead from a pet-shop and buy half an amulet. The amulet complete confers the heart's desire; the children travel into the past, to periods and places in ancient history, in search of the lost half.

The Enchanted Castle 1907

Gerald, Jimmy and Kathleen, staying at school during the holidays under the care of the French mistress, find their way into the grounds of a castle. They meet Mabel, the housekeeper's niece, and find a ring which makes them invisible. They have adventures with the ring and other enchantments of the castle.

The Magic City 1910

Philip and Lucy shrink to the size of the city Philip built and live among its curious inhabitants. A disagreeable Nurse also finds her way in and competes with Philip for the throne of the city.

Wet Magic 1913

Francis, Mavis, Bernard and Kathleen rescue a mermaid from a sea-side fair. They go to the country of the Merfolk and help them in their struggle against the uncouth Underfolk.

3. HISTORICAL FANTASIES

The House of Arden 1908

Edred and Elfrida Arden search for the lost family treasure in past English history, conveyed by the magic of the white Mouldiwarp. They never quite find it, but instead bring home their supposedly dead father by magic.

Harding's Luck 1909

The story of Edred and Elfrida's cousin Dickie, also a traveller in time. In the present a lame slum child, he is an Arden of wealth and noble birth in the past. He returns to the present for the sake of his companion, the tramp Beale, and sets about reforming him. Dickie is found to be the real Lord Arden, and the family treasure is discovered. Finally he goes back to the past for good, so as not to deprive his uncle and cousins of the Arden inheritance.

BIBLIOGRAPHY

A Bibliography of
E. Nesbit's Children's Books

This is a revised version of the bibliography that appeared in *Magic and the Magician* by Noel Streatfeild (Ernest Benn, 1958). I am most indebted to Ernest Benn Ltd, and to Mr Roger Lancelyn Green for their help in the revision of this list.

Some Tales in Collections, Raphael Tuck & Son, 1893-4
Some Tales in Collections, Ernest Nister, various dates
Pussy Tales. Illustrated by Lucy Kemp-Welch, Marcus Ward & Co, 1895
Doggy Tales. Illustrated by Lucy Kemp-Welch, Marcus Ward & Co, 1895.
As Happy as a King. Illustrated by S. Rosamund Praeger, Marcus Ward & Co, 1896
The Children's Shakespeare. Edited by Edric Vredenburg, Raphael Tuck & Son, 1897
Royal Children of English History, Raphael Tuck & Son, 1897
A Book of Dogs. Illustrated by Winifred Austin, J. M. Dent & Co, 1898
The Story of the Treasure Seekers. Illustrated by Gordon Browne and Lewis Baumer, T. Fisher Unwin, 1899
  Reset edition with original illustrations, Ernest Benn, 1958
  Published in the United States of America by Coward-McCann Inc.
  New edition. Illustrated by Cecil Leslie, Penguin, 1958
  Nonesuch Cygnet edition (with *The Wouldbegoods*). Introduced by Noel Streatfeild and illustrated by Susan Einzig, Nonesuch Press, 1966
Pussy and Doggy Tales. Illustrated by Lucy Kemp-Welch, J. M. Dent & Co, 1899
The Book of Dragons. Illustrated by H. R. Millar with decorations by H. Granville Fell, Harper Bros, 1900
Nine Unlikely Tales for Children. Illustrated by H. R. Millar and Claude Shepperson, T. Fisher Unwin, 1901
  Latest impression, Ernest Benn, 1938

The Wouldbegoods. Illustrated by Arthur H. Buckland and John
Hassall, T. Fisher Unwin, 1901

Reset edition with original illustrations, Ernest Benn, 1958

Published in the United States of America by Coward-McCann
Inc.

New edition. Illustrated by Cecil Leslie, Penguin, 1958

Nonesuch Cygnet edition (with *The Story of The Treasure
Seekers*). Introduced by Noel Streatfeild and illustrated by
Susan Einzig, Nonesuch Press, 1966

Five Children and It. Illustrated by H. R. Millar, T. Fisher Unwin, 1902

Reset edition with original illustrations, Ernest Benn, 1957

Published in the United States of America by Coward-McCann
Inc.

New edition with original illustrations, Penguin, 1959

The Revolt of the Toys or What Comes of Quarrelling, two stories.
Illustrated by Ambrose Dudley, Ernest Nister, 1902

The Rainbow Queen and Other Stories. Illustrated by E. and
N. R. Taylor, M. Bowley, etc, Raphael Tuck & Son, 1903

The Phoenix and the Carpet. Illustrated by H. R. Millar, George
Newnes, 1904

Facsimile of first edition, Ernest Benn, 1956

Published in the United States of America by Coward-McCann
Inc.

New edition with original illustrations, Penguin, 1959

New Treasure Seekers. Illustrated by Gordon Browne and Lewis
Baumer, T. Fisher Unwin, 1904

Reset edition. Illustrated by C. Walter Hodges, Ernest Benn,
1949

Published in the United States of America by Coward-McCann
Inc.

Cat Tales. Illustrated by Isabel Watkin, Ernest Nister, 1904

Oswald Bastable and Others. Illustrated by C. E. Brock and H. R.
Millar, Wells, Gardner, Darton & Co, 1905

Peter Pugg. Illustrated by Harry Rowntree and John Hassall,
Alfred Cooke, 1905

The Story of the Amulet. Illustrated by H. R. Millar, T. Fisher
Unwin, 1906

Reset edition with original illustrations, Ernest Benn, 1957

Published in the United States of America by Coward-McCann Inc.

New edition with original illustrations, Penguin, 1959

The Railway Children. Illustrated by C. E. Brock, Wells, Gardner, Darton & Co, 1906

The Enchanted Castle. Illustrated by H. R. Millar, T. Fisher Unwin, 1907

Facsimile of first edition, Ernest Benn, 1957

Published in the United States of America by Coward-McCann Inc.

Reset edition. Illustrated by Lynton Lamb, Ernest Benn, 1957

The Old Nursery Stories (No. 1 of the Children's Bookcase series). Illustrated by W. H. Margetson, edited by E. Nesbit, Henry Frowde and Hodder & Stoughton, 1908-11

The House of Arden. Illustrated by H. R. Millar, T. Fisher Unwin 1908

Reset edition. Illustrated by Desmond E. Walduck, Ernest Benn, 1949

Published in the United States of America by Coward-McCann Inc.

Harding's Luck. Illustrated by H. R. Millar, Hodder & Stoughton, 1909

Reset edition. Illustrated by Desmond E. Walduck, Ernest Benn, 1949

Published in the United States of America by Coward-McCann Inc.

The Magic City. Illustrated by H. R. Millar, Macmillan & Co, 1910

Latest impression, Ernest Benn, 1958

Published in the United States of America by Coward-McCann Inc.

The Wonderful Garden, or The Three C's. Illustrated by H. R. Millar, Macmillan & Co, 1911

Latest impression, Ernest Benn, 1959

Published in the United States of America by Coward-McCann Inc.

The Magic World. Illustrated by H. R. Millar and Spencer Pryse, Macmillan & Co, 1912

Latest impression, Ernest Benn, 1959

Published in the United States of America by Coward-McCann
Inc.

Wet Magic. Illustrated by H. R. Millar, T. Werner Laurie, 1913
Latest impression, Ernest Benn, 1958
Published in the United States of America by Coward-McCann
Inc.

Five of Us—And Madeline. Illustrated by Norah S. Unwin, T.
Fisher Unwin, 1925
Reset edition. Illustrated by Peter Freeman, Ernest Benn, 1958
Published in the United States of America by Coward-McCann
Inc.

Complete History of the Bastable Family. Illustrated by Gordon
Browne, Lewis Baumer, Arthur H. Buckland & John Hassall,
Ernest Benn, 1928

Howard Pyle

ELIZABETH NESBITT

ACKNOWLEDGMENTS

I am greatly indebted to the wonderfully complete bibliography, *Howard Pyle; A Record of His Illustrations and Writings*, compiled by Willard S. Morse and Gertrude Brinckle.

To the staffs of the Boys' and Girls' Division, the Reference Department and the Fine Arts Division of the Carnegie Library of Pittsburgh I extend my thanks for the help given me. My thanks are also due Mr Frederick R. Goff of the Rare Book Division of The Library of Congress.

I am deeply grateful for the hospitality and expert help given me by Miss Virginia Haviland, Head of the Children's Book Section of the General Reference and Bibliography Division of the Reference Department of The Library of Congress and by her staff.

It was a privilege to visit the Howard Pyle Rooms of the Delaware Art Center in Wilmington, Delaware, and to examine the Thornton Oakley Collection of Howard Pyle Materials in the Rare Book Department of The Free Library of Philadelphia, Pennsylvania.

E.N.

CONTENTS

L

1. Howard Pyle: 'An Illuminating Joyfulness in Beautiful Things'

In front of the house in Wilmington, Delaware, where Howard Pyle lived as a child, was a green lawn, with a terraced bank. Beyond could be seen the turnpike, down which, now and then, would pass a train of Conestoga wagons, a sight which filled the boy with wonder. On the other side of the house was a garden. The memory of the beauty of this garden was to remain with him all his life long, and was to be reflected in the descriptions of the gardens in his books, *The Garden Behind the Moon*, *The Story of Jack Ballister's Fortunes*, and in some of the descriptive passages in the Arthurian retellings. Inside the house was a library with a fireplace, where hickory logs burned. On the hearth rug before the fire, the boy lay for many an hour, revelling in the good books his mother loved, and in the illustrations of Bewick and Darley and Tenniel, and the pictures in *Punch*.

It is little wonder that Pyle, recalling his childhood environment with warm and loving detail in a brief autobiographical sketch published in *The Woman's Home Companion* for April, 1912, should speak of the 'illuminating joyfulness in beautiful things which brightened my childhood'.*

It is easy to trace the relationship between the influences exerted on him in his childhood, and the kind and quality of his work as illustrator and writer. His total career was shaped first of all, of course, by his twin talents, but secondly and

---

* Howard Pyle, 'When I Was a Little Boy', *The Woman's Home Companion*, Vol. 39, p. 5 (April, 1912).

importantly, by his early surroundings and by a few incidents so timely and determining that it is difficult to believe
that they were as fortuitous as they must have been.

Howard Pyle was born in Wilmington, in the state of
Delaware, on March 5, 1853, the son of William and
Margaret Churchman Pyle. Both parents were of Quaker
stock; his first American ancestor on his father's side was
Robert Pyle, who came to America with William Penn's
company in 1682. William and Margaret Pyle were hospitable to people and ideas and Wilmington was a city which
offered them much in intellectual and cultural pursuits and
in the stimulation afforded through the city's interest in
current issues and in new ideas. It was a place which looked
back with pride and affection upon its history and tradition,
and at the same time one which looked forward, with intellectual curiosity, to many new developments in literature and
art, and in social reform.

Howard Pyle's childhood education was in private schools.
He attended the Friends' School in Wilmington, and later a
school conducted by Thomas Clarkson Taylor. He seems to
have been a quiet boy, one who got along well with companions of his own age, but who also could be equally happy
by himself. In spite of the capacity for detailed research he
revealed in his adult life, he seems to have had little real love
of study as a child or as an adolescent. Indeed there is no
doubt that his home life had much greater impact upon him
than his school life had. His mother must have been a
uniquely interesting person, and throughout her life, her
influence upon him was very real. It was she who introduced
him to the books he loved so well, the Grimm fairy tales, the
stories from the *Arabian Nights*, *Robinson Crusoe*, *Gulliver's
Travels*, *A Wonder Book* and *Tanglewood Tales*, *Pilgrim's
Progress*, and *Slovenly Peter*. She transmitted to him her

unusual appreciation of the significance and beauty of folk literature. She aroused in him an early interest in Robin Hood by reading to him Ritson's collection of ballads, and *Percy's Reliques of Ancient English Poetry*. His interest in illustration stemmed from her love of pictures, especially pictures in books.

When at the age of sixteen, or thereabouts, he showed no interest in college, it was his mother who encouraged him to study art. For three years, he attended a small school conducted by a Mr Van der Weilen, a Belgian artist who combined a knowledge of technique with unusual teaching ability. These years of study do not appear to have given Pyle any strong sense of direction as to his future career. In addition, straitened family finances forced him to work in his father's leather business. At the same time, he became absorbed in social activities in Wilmington. Nevertheless, the years under Van der Weilen, a rigorous and demanding teacher who gave individual attention to his students, provided Pyle with a solid foundation in the technique of drawing. The choice of this school was one of those happy incidents which had a disproportionate influence on his later career.

In 1876, there occurred another chance incident which had an even more decisive effect. In the spring of that year, he had visited Chincoteague, an island lying off the coast of Virginia. Here his interest had been caught by the capturing of the wild ponies, this being a major occupation of the people of the island. He was also intrigued by the character of the people, and by the whole atmosphere of the island. After his return to Wilmington, he wrote and illustrated an article on Chincoteague. The writing revealed the eye for picture-making detail which was to be so strong a characteristic of his later work. At the urging of his mother, he sent the article to *Scribner's Monthly*, which accepted it. Scribners were particularly impressed by the illustrations, and advised Pyle that he should consider coming to New York to write and illustrate for magazines. This advice seemed to him and his family so good that he and they were willing to make any sacrifice to enable him to spend some time in New York. So, in October, 1876, he left Wilmington, with the promise of financial help from his family, should he need it.

The three years he spent in New York were important ones in relation to his professional and his personal life. This importance is revealed most clearly in the letters written to his mother, many of which are quoted at length by his biographer, Charles D. Abbot. They give detailed pictures of his life, his work, his reading, his friends, his enjoyment of the theatre when he could afford it. Most of all, they reveal Pyle himself, the romanticism which was so inherent a quality, the versatility of his imagination, the response to the spirit of folk literature, to its ways of expression, to its humour and wisdom. And always he seems to have thought of stories in terms of pictures, of the illustrations which a story or any piece of literature would inspire. In a letter written to his mother on November 24, 1876, he asked her to lend him her copy of *Percy's Reliques*.

'I have been thinking lately that stories from the life of Robin Hood might be an interesting thing for *St Nicholas* —And then how gloriously they would illustrate.'*

(And how gloriously they were illustrated when *The Merry Adventures of Robin Hood* was published in 1883.)

A letter dated two days later is interesting in its indication of his reading in folk literature.

* From a letter quoted in Charles D. Abbott, *Howard Pyle, A Chronicle*, Harper, N.Y. 1925, p. 31.

'I took Thorp's *Northern Mythology* out of the Mercantile library . . . It is a rich mine to select from, although a dull book to read . . . I shall make note of a great many (stories) . . . Some of the stories of trolls and kaboutermannekins are funny in the extreme and could be woven with some shaping into amusing and quaint stories.'*

This tendency to visualise his reading and the equally persistent habit of thinking of writing and illustration as inseparable were possible contributing factors to the conflict in his mind as to whether writing or illustration should be his chosen career. There were other reasons for his uncertainty on this point. His mother felt strongly that his greater talent lay in the field of art. He himself felt that when he wrote, he was often selfconscious, stiff, and unable to express his thoughts and ideas with ease and fluency. Nevertheless he persisted in his belief that there was in him a latent ability to write.

His first work in New York was a combination of writing and illustrating, short animal fables illustrated in line. These were published with some frequency in *St Nicholas*. This magazine for children had been established in 1873, and under the inspired and expert editorship of Mary Mapes Dodge was rapidly becoming famous as a primary influence in the improvement of children's literature in the United States. In the April, 1877, issue of *St Nicholas* appeared Pyle's first fairy tale, 'Hans Gottenlieb the Fiddler.' The source for this story was one of the legends in Thorp's *Northern Mythology* and the tale as he wrote it had been outlined in the letter written to his mother in the late fall of 1876.

The pay for his illustrated fables was not high—approxi-

* From a letter written to his mother dated November 26, 1876, quoted in Charles D. Abbott, *op. cit.*, p. 93.

mately two and a half dollars for each fable—and *St Nicholas* reasonably could accept only a certain number of them. The limiting of this market and his financial need heightened the always present question as to whether he should concentrate on painting, illustration, and drawing as a career. After much hesitation, and with many lingering doubts, he decided that his greater ability lay in this field. He rented a studio, and began intensive work on picture after picture. He had plenty of ideas, fertility of imagination, and originality of conception, and as he worked, he began to develop the highly individual methods that were to set him apart from other artists.

At this time, Charles Parsons was art editor for Harper and Brothers. He had selected and trained a group of young illustrators, among them Edwin Austin Abbey, Arthur Burdett Frost, and Charles Stanley Reinhart, who were improving the art of illustration to a degree of excellence hitherto unknown in America. Mr Parsons accepted several of the sketches Pyle submitted to him. However, Parsons' high standards made him sceptical as to the standard of the technical aspect of Pyle's work, with the result that he invariably required that one of his staff artists should redraw the picture on wood for reproduction purposes. This was not calculated to make Pyle happy, and his dissatisfaction finally gave him the courage to plead with Parsons that he be allowed to complete the work on a sketch which he called 'The Wreck in the Offing'. This is a picture of a group of life-savers or coast guardsmen, playing cards around a table. In the midst of the game, one of their fellows, his coat and hat streaming with water, throws open the door to announce that a ship has been wrecked in the offing. The picture is full of action and arrested action. The art editor finally agreed to Pyle's request, and Pyle worked on the picture for six weeks. At the end of that time, still unsatisfied with the results, but reduced to his last five cents, he submitted the drawing. There is something very touching in his later description of his sudden realisation that the decision of the editor might well have a binding result on his future; of the blending of hope and despair with which he awaited the decision, and of the almost equally unbearable relief when Parsons not only agreed to use the picture, but to make a double-page spread of it. And there is something very young and ingratiating in his celebration of the occasion with a party. He was right in his instinctive feeling that acceptance or rejection of the picture would mark a turning point in his life. 'The Wreck in the Offing' was published in *Harper's Weekly* for March 9, 1878, and the results of its publication were several. The picture was praised by artists, acclaimed by the public, and brought Pyle's work to the attention of publishers. His illustrations and independent pictures began to appear in all the best periodicals of the day. He had as much work as he could handle. From a personal point of view, not the least pleasant of the effects of the quality of the picture was the fact that it brought him the friendship of many young artists of the day, of Winslow Homer, Edwin Abbey, and most of all, of A. B. Frost.

By late in 1879, Pyle began to feel that he had absorbed all that New York could offer him. He had gained skill and a knowledge of technique; he had established a reputation which assured him of plentiful work; and his thoughts were again turning to his never completely abandoned desire to write. In addition, the circle of friends whose companionship had meant much to him, was gradually breaking up. Abbey was in England, and Frost had moved to Philadelphia. So he decided to return to Wilmington, having made arrangements with Harper's that stories and articles should be sent to him for illustration, and that he should be considered a regular member of the staff.

In 1880, he became engaged to Anne Poole, of Wilmington, and in April of 1881 they were married, with A. B. Frost as best man. There is every evidence that he and his wife created for their large family a childhood as happy and memorable as was his own.

Descriptions of him at this and later periods of his life consistently mention certain physical attributes. He was a tall man, well built, clean shaven, with a high forehead and a serene and friendly expression. Photographs of him which constitute part of the exhibits in the Howard Pyle section of the Delaware Art Center in Wilmington bear out these written descriptions, and reveal him as a man of distinctive appearance. So often, in attempting to capture the inner quality of the man, the simple, fine old word 'good' is resorted to by those who knew him. Somehow, in the contexts in which the word is used, contexts which denote wholesomeness, sanity, sweetness, and integrity, the word leaves an impression of greatness and nobility of character not likely to be achieved by more pretentious words or more elaborate character analysis.

After his marriage, his illustrating and writing showed in intense degree those characteristics so often remarked upon: quality, quantity, and a variety of interests substantiated by amazingly intensive, detailed study. Dilettantism would have been abhorrent to him. His knowledge of American history, especially of the Colonial and Revolutionary periods, was so exact in its detail that it is said of him that he knew the number of buttons on the uniform of an officer of a definite regiment, the colour of the hat worn by General Wolfe at Quebec, in what battles specific regiments fought. His insistence upon accuracy of detail in illustration was accompanied by an equal insistence upon the interpretative power of illustration. He was in constant demand as an illustrator, especially in the fields of American and medieval history.

In the midst of illustrating articles and books by others, and of writing and illustrating stories and articles of his own, he had never forgotten his particular interest in writing for children. In 1883, *The Merry Adventures of Robin Hood of Great Renown in Nottinghamshire* was published. It is considered by many the most beautiful example of Pyle's twin talents as author-illustrator. Definitely its publication established him as one of America's foremost writers and illustrators for children.

He had never lost the love and understanding of fairy tales which was one of the greatest gifts his mother gave him. The pages of *St Nicholas* and *Harper's Young People* are filled with fairy tales written by him. The first of his collections of original fairy tales, *Pepper and Salt or Seasoning for Young Folks*, appeared in 1886. These stories had been published previously in *Harper's Young People*, a recently established magazine for children. *Pepper and Salt* was followed in 1888 by *The Wonder Clock or Four and Twenty Marvellous Tales, Being One For Each Hour of the Day*, and in 1895, by his last collection of this kind of story, *Twilight Land*. Stories in the last two books had also been published in *Harper's Young People*. His only book length fairy tale, *The Garden Behind the Moon*, appeared in the same year as *Twilight Land*.

His interest in history turned his attention to the writing of historical fiction for children. *Otto of the Silver Hand* was published in the same year as *The Wonder Clock*. Four years later, in 1892, his second story of the Middle Ages, *Men of Iron*, was published in book form, having

been first published serially in *Harper's Young People*.
One of the manifestations of his mother's spiritual and
poetic temperament was the mysticism which led her to
adopt the doctrines of Swedenborg. Pyle shared with her an
affinity for the mystical, a sense of the symbolical. These
traits, together with his innate understanding of the whole
character of the Middle Ages, made consideration of the
retelling of the Arthurian romances almost inevitable.
No doubt his interest was fortified by the success of *Robin
Hood* and encouraged by the many suggestions that he do
for King Arthur what he had done for Robin Hood. In 1902
he suggested to Scribners that he retell the adventures of
King Arthur and his knights. Scribners were enthusiastic
about the idea, and Pyle began the colossal job of investiga-
tion, study, and reading of the great mass of Arthurian
material. The original plan of three volumes was expanded to
four. The first instalment of *The Story of King Arthur and
His Knights* came out in the November, 1902, issue of
St Nicholas, the last in the October, 1903, number. The book
itself was published in 1903, its length 312 pages, a long book
by any standards. The other three books, of roughly the
same size, were spread over the next seven years: *The Story
of the Champions of the Round Table* in 1905; *The Story of
Sir Launcelot and His Companions* in 1907; and *The Story
of the Grail and The Passing of Arthur* in 1910. It is astonishing that so massive a task of reading, organisation, writing,
and illustration—for each book was lavishly illustrated and
decorated—could have been accomplished in seven years.

Many summers were spent by the Pyle family in Rehoboth, a seaside town south of Cape Henlopen. These
summers were happy and relaxed, cherished by the whole
family. For Pyle, they generated another interest, a strangely
compelling one. To the north of Rehoboth are immense sand

dunes which legend says were hiding places for pirate booty. These legends held much attraction for Pyle, probably appealing to the romanticism which was so much a part of him. However, a statement written by him under one of his pirate pictures, 'Ye Pirate Bold', implies another reason for the fascination which the subject of piracy had for him, and reveals another aspect of his character.

'It is not because of his life of adventure and daring that I admire this one of my favourite heroes; nor is it because of blowing winds nor blue ocean nor palmy islands which he knew so well; nor is it because of the gold he spent nor treasure he had. He was a man who knew his own mind and what he wanted.'*

Perhaps the last sentence explains many things about Pyle; his intense application and enormous capacity for work, once he knew his own mind in relation to his career; the originality and unconventionality of his theories of art and illustration; his distrust of the influence of Europe on American art. His beliefs were firm, his ideas the results of long thought and experimentation, his standards exacting, and he spared himself least of all in the execution of his ideas and his pursuit of excellence.

He went into the subject of pirates with characteristic un-flagging zeal. His library contained almost every book dealing with the lives and exploits of such famous or infamous characters as Morgan, Kidd, and Teach. As always, his interest found expression in the forms of illustration and writing. Many of his illustrations and paintings of pirates are masterpieces and brought him tremendous acclaim. There is one of a pirate captain lying dead upon the shore which the painter and illustrator Frederic Remington admired so much that he asked Pyle to give it to him. 'It is

* Abbott, *op. cit.*, p. 151.

simply all-fired satisfying,' Remington said. Pirate-lore also provided the stimulus for articles, short stories, two adult novels, and a book for young people, *The Story of Jack Ballister's Fortunes*, which was published serially in *St Nicholas*, and in book form in 1895.

After Pyle's death, a friend, Merle Johnson, collected a large group of Pyle's articles, stories, and illustrations on pirates, and published them under the title of *Howard Pyle's Book of Pirates*. The success of this compilation led to the later publication of *Howard Pyle's Book of the American Spirit*, a collection of his illustrations in the field of American history, with a descriptive text taken from original sources, edited by Francis J. Dowd.

At the age of forty-one Pyle turned to a teaching career which was to last the rest of his life and which was to have an influence on American illustration equal to, if not greater than, the influence exerted by his own work.

In the fall of 1894, he began to teach a class in illustration at the Drexel Institute of Arts and Sciences in Philadelphia. He had always disagreed with the methods used at that time in schools of art. This disagreement and his own experience had developed theories of illustration unorthodox in his time, which are provocative and fascinating, but which belong properly to the discussion of him as an artist. He anticipated teaching with eager interest, hoping to demonstrate the validity of his ideas. At the end of his first year, his success was such that he was even then considered one of the best teachers of illustration in America. Eventually he worked out an arduous schedule. He went to Philadelphia two days a week. In the mornings he worked individually with the students; in the afternoons he lectured; and in the evenings he gave additional time to advanced students.

In 1898, with the co-operation of Drexel Institute, he

established a summer class at Chadd's Ford, Pennsylvania, where the Pyles now had a summer home. Drexel Institute undertook to give scholarships to a selected number of promising artists; Pyle agreed to give instruction without salary.

In 1900, he resigned from Drexel for several reasons. Chiefly, he felt that in a class so large, there were only a few who had the creative artistic potential to profit from the intensive, specialised instruction he preferred to give. If he gave particular attention to these few, he would be unfair to others in the class. In addition, he had conceived another plan, very dear to him. This plan called for the building of a studio in Wilmington next to his own. There he planned to teach and supervise the work of about six to nine pupils, selected from art schools all over the country. The students would pay only a small sum to cover the interest on the investment in the building, the heating of the building, and fees for any models necessary. Most of the members of the first class came from his classes at Drexel. But in 1903, he received between two and three hundred applications from all over the United States. Of these, he accepted only three.

Many of his students at Chadd's Ford and Wilmington became famous in their own right . . . Maxfield Parrish, N. C. Wyeth, Elizabeth Shippen Green, Jessie Willcox Smith, Thornton Oakley, Violet Oakley, Harvey Dunn, Stanley Arthur, Frank Schoonover, W. J. Aylward.

His teaching was time-consuming and exhausting, because he never gave it less than his best. But the rewards were great. He wrote the President of Drexel:

'I know of no better legacy a man can leave to the world than that he had aided others to labour at an art so beautiful as that to which I have devoted my life.'*

* Abbott, *op. cit.*, p. 207.

All his life Pyle had refused to entertain any suggestion that he visit Europe and become acquainted with the originals of European masterpieces. His stubbornness on this point was linked up with his theories on illustration and his belief that America had been too dependent upon European methods and must develop her own indigenous art. He held these views in spite of the fact that some of his own work was influenced to some extent by German artists, and particularly by Dürer, as Joseph Pennell and others have pointed out. It is also true that many of his illustrations dealt with European scenes and backgrounds which he had never seen, as Joseph Pennell again, and rather caustically, mentions in his comment on the Robin Hood illustrations.

Towards the end of his life (he died at the relatively early age of fifty-eight) his new work in mural painting changed his mind as to the values of a first-hand knowledge of European art. At the turn of the century, there was in America an upsurge of interest in mural decoration for new public buildings. Pyle had been commissioned to do several murals which were highly successful. He felt that there was much similarity between book illustration and mural painting, saying that the chief difference lay in the substitution of a very large flat decorated surface for a small one. His interest in this kind of painting became so strong that he was convinced he must go to Italy to see for himself the work of the masters, and particularly their use of colour.

He sailed from New York in November of 1910, with his family and his secretary. His health had begun to show the results of long years of work so intense as to put too great a strain on even his remarkable vitality, energy, and enthusiasm. When he reached Italy, he was ill and depressed, and recurring periods of sickness robbed him of strength. In spite of his increasing weakness, he found great joy in the work of the old masters, particularly in the colour they used, saying in a letter to a friend that these paintings made him feel that he was surrounded by a glow of soft, warm colour, and that he did not see how any human being could have painted as they did. He found Florence in the spring-time exceedingly beautiful. A hot, tiring trip to Genoa brought another period of illness. Later in the summer, he was able to travel to Siena, where his health seemed to improve. But on his return to Florence, he became seriously ill. On November 9, 1911, almost a year from the time he sailed from New York, he died.

II. The Illustrator

In the mid nineteenth century, illustration was not recognised in America as an acknowledged and legitimate fine art. Such illustration as existed belonged to the 'graveyard' school, characterised by a sickly sentimentality, empty elegance, and a lifeless if accurate representation of every detail. To this generalisation there were a few exceptions, notably the work of Felix Octavius Carr Darley who illustrated a number of books between the 1840s and the 1880s. But his illustrations for James Fenimore Cooper's novels, Washington Irving's legends, editions of *Hans Brinker* and *A Visit from St Nicholas*, and other titles, were so good as to be non-typical of the time.

By the time Pyle went to New York in 1876, ideas had begun to change and movements were under way which were to have a vital effect upon illustration in general and possibly upon Pyle in particular. The word 'possibly' is used deliberately, because he himself was an influence greater than any influence exerted upon him. It is difficult to believe that the vigour and originality of his ideas and performance would have been lessened even if the years he spent in New York had not coincided with the developments which were to produce a new look in American illustration. On the other hand, it is undoubtedly true that he began his work at the right time, in the right place, and under the right conditions, and in association with a congenial group of young artists.

The last quarter of the nineteenth century in America was a period when the magazine achieved prominence and when it had great influence on literature and art. This was very true of magazines for children. Books which have become classics and standards for children appeared first in such periodicals as *The Riverside Magazine for Young People*, *Our Young Folks*, *St Nicholas*, and *Harper's Young People*. The editors of these, and of magazines for adults, realising the part played by illustrations in attracting a wider audience, did their utmost to discover and develop artistic talent. A. W. Drake, art editor of *Scribner's Monthly*, and Charles Parsons, art director of Harper and Brothers, were particularly vigorous in this respect, bringing together groups of young artists many of whom, like Edwin Abbey, A. B. Frost, Frederic Remington, and Howard Pyle, were to become famous.

During the same period, reproductive processes improved. Photo-engraving methods developed in the '70s and '80s made possible much greater freedom for the artist. Relieved of the necessity for the detailed line work required for cutting in wood, he could now draw in any medium, on any scale, and the illustration could be reproduced effectively by the photographic process. The relief afforded to the artist by the improved methods of reproduction may be gauged by the discouragement Pyle felt when some of his early drawings for fables published in *St Nicholas* were criticised. Upon being reduced, the lines became heavy and coarse, and the illustrations, in Pyle's own words, cheap-looking. It is no wonder that more faithful reproduction of original drawings not only encouraged artists, but also stimulated them to greater freedom in the development of their talents, and encouraged them in their refusal to use the rigid, prescribed, and unrealistic form of illustration demanded by the sentimental school of art. Nevertheless, previous ideas died hard, and much of the new illustration received at first severe contemporary criticism.

In the light of these stirrings in the world of art, there can be no doubt that the years in New York provided for Pyle a climate most favourable to the development of his genius. He worked there under the encouragement of so progressive and knowledgeable a man as Charles Parsons; the atmosphere of new ideas and methods was congenial to him; and the companionship of his fellow artists was in itself a stimulus.

There are three reasons for his own final pre-eminence as a person of immeasurable influence on American illustration. These are his theories of illustration, the impact of his illustrations in themselves, and the far reaching results of his teaching.

Pyle's theories of illustration, as has been said, are highly interesting and provocative. They emerge most clearly in letters written to friends, artists, editors, and to authors whose books he illustrated. His arguments are persuasive, and the examples he gives telling, so that he usually convinced his correspondent.

His central belief in regard to illustration was that the artist should illustrate the feeling the author conveys, rather than a precise incident or scene mentioned in the text. If the illustrator is confined to the mere depicting of an event he is restricted and hampered. The two arts, writing and illustrating should, in Pyle's words, 'round the circle instead of advancing in parallel lines upon which it is almost impossible to keep them abreast.' Pictorial art should represent some point of view that carries over the whole significance of a situation. It should convey an image of the meaning of the text. Therefore, in illustrating a book, it is preferable to choose for an illustration, some point descriptive of the text, but not necessarily mentioned in the text.

Illustration is then something more than the skilful

representation of a fact; it is rather an expression of an ideal. The expression of an ideal can be achieved only if pictures are creations of the imagination. Pyle did not minimise the need for mastery of technique, but he did place the development of the imagination first. He claimed that a man is not a creative artist because of clever technique or method. He is an artist only when he is able to sense the inner significance of things and to convey that significance to the minds of others. The quality of imagination cannot be given by one person to another; but where it exists, its development should be encouraged, rather than 'stifled by a hard incrustation of academic methods.' His strong feeling on this point led him to distrust the methods of art instruction in art schools at home and abroad. It also led him to disapprove a too slavish use of models. Indeed, he claimed, or seems to claim, that in some pictures, the artist must be dependent completely on his imagination, since it is impossible for a model to be posed in and to hold certain positions. The originality of these ideas must, of course, be determined in relation to the time in which Pyle lived, a time when accepted theory was the reverse of his, when technique was the major emphasis, when schools advocated the drawing from models, and when illustration was considered to be a stepchild of the fine arts, if indeed it belonged to the fine arts at all.

In his own work, as in his theories of illustration, Pyle was an originator, acknowledgedly the most outstanding illustrator of the late nineteenth and early twentieth centuries in America. His originality extended beyond illustration to his conception of total book design. He understood the importance of beauty and harmony in every detail of the make-up of a book, and in this respect, as in so many others, he set standards which have permanent value. It is appreciation of this understanding of his which leads so many to regret the changes made in the 1946 edition of *The Merry Adventures of Robin Hood*. In this edition, published from the original drawings found in Charles Scribner's library after his death, the decorations which originally surrounded the drawings were omitted because it was felt that they lessened the strength of the drawings and were dated, being typical of the Victorian period. They were typical of Pyle, and of the beauty of his total design. Without these decorations, the pictures seem bald; something vital to the total effect has been removed.

Joseph Pennell, in his *Pen Drawing and Pen Draughtsmen*, says that among the books by Howard Pyle which every student of art should know are *Robin Hood, Pepper and Salt, The Wonder Clock,* and *Otto of the Silver Hand.* N. C. Wyeth would undoubtedly have added the four volumes of Arthurian romance, which he considered outstanding.

All these are illustrated with pen and ink drawings. Many art critics have pointed out the similarities between Pyle's work in this style and that of Dürer. Certainly the similarities are there, but there is also much that is uniquely Pyle. His line drawings are so exquisitely harmonious with the contents of the books, so interpretative of the spirits of the books, that they have always overshadowed the half tones which he used later to illustrate *Men of Iron, The Garden Behind the Moon,* and *The Story of Jack Ballister's Fortunes.* It would be hard to say that they overshadow the magnificent imaginative quality and the dramatic colour of his pirate pictures. The preference for his pen drawings, on the part of laymen as well as artists and critics, is in large part due to the fact that these pictures and the texts they illustrate are interdependent, each contributing to the completeness and perfection of the whole, and thereby conforming with fine exactitude, to Pyle's leading theory of illustration.

His first illustrations of this kind, accompanying the fables published in *St Nicholas* in the late 1870s, show qualities new in illustration for children, in spite of the fact that poor reproduction to some extent diminished these qualities; they had a freshness, a wholesomeness, a strength, and a gaiety so different from the vacuousness of most that had gone before that they must have been startling.

Implicitly present in his earliest published drawings, these characteristics and others were fully realised in the illustrations in the books he wrote later. The illustrations for *Pepper and Salt* and *The Wonder Clock* are so matchless in their realisation of the fairy tales in the books that it is impossible to think separately of the pictures and the stories. An adult, turning over the pages of these two books, finds with incredulous astonishment that the spell has worked again. Without conscious effort, he has become a child, at home in the world of the folk tale, soaked in its atmosphere, breathing its spirit. In Pyle's pictures, it is a storied world. The pictures are alive with movement and action, full of detail which in itself has storytelling quality. They are peopled with folk tale characters who, by reason of Pyle's skilful and imaginative pen, are quickened into life, animate, breathing representations of their prototypes in folk tales; kings and queens, beautiful princesses and handsome princes, rotund, shrewd, and cheerful peasants, gentle maidens, the gooseherd surrounded by his curious geese, sly and wicked foxes, elves, gnomes, boggarts, all enchantingly true to character. There is in the pictures in these books, as there is even more strikingly in the later illustrations for the Arthurian books, a lovely, haunting atmosphere in the glimpses of castles, towers, and quaint villages. Head pieces, tail pieces, decorated initial letters, add immeasurably to the total beauty of design and at the same time enhance Pyle's lovingly sympathetic and sincere recreation of the flavourful spirit of folk literature. Adequate appreciation of the fineness of the illustrations in *Pepper and Salt* and *The Wonder Clock* can be attained only by browsing through earlier printings. In later printings, the necessity for using worn plates has dimmed the original beauty of the drawings.

In his last collection of fairy tales, *Twilight Land*, he also used line drawings. These, however, do not have the forcefulness, the outstanding folk quality, the impressiveness of detail, which so distinguish the illustrations for *Pepper and Salt* and *The Wonder Clock*.

The Merry Adventures of Robin Hood is thought by many to be Pyle's most perfect book. Perhaps it is the one he himself took greatest pride in, since he once said that it was the only one of his books that might become a classic. It was the book which was longest in the making. Seven years elapsed between the time, in 1876, when he wrote to his mother about his idea of retelling for children the Robin Hood ballads and the publication of the book in 1883. His feeling for this book may have been influenced by the great praise it received, in England as well as in America. Joseph Pennell said that it made a tremendous impression when it appeared in England, even upon William Morris, who had been of the belief that nothing good, artistically, could come from America. There is legitimate reason for the acclaim the book received. What N. C. Wyeth called the 'compelling force of decorative craftsmanship' is explicitly demonstrated in the line drawings and decorations in the *Robin Hood*. The full page pictures, the vignettes, the decorated initials seem to grow out of the printed page, print and decoration becoming integrated parts of the whole. The entire make-up of the book is fully consistent with Pyle's belief that the arts of writing and illustration should round the circle. Equally consistent with his theories is the manner in which the illustrations convey the spirit of England and of these ballad stories, their vital, joyous, zestful quality. No one can argue the truth of Joseph Pennell's remark, that here Pyle created beautiful pictures of a country he had never seen. It is probable that Pyle had no intention of depicting, realistically and accurately, English landscape. Indeed he implies as much in his introduction to the *Robin Hood*. His intent was rather to draw upon his imagination, to idealise the landscape in keeping with the spirit which breathes in the stories.

The pen and ink drawings for his volumes of Arthurian stories show a comprehension of the subtlety, of the complexities of character, mood, and emotion, of the depth of human passions characteristic of the medieval romances and very different from the straightforwardness, the simple objectivity of the folk tale, and the frank, uncomplicated joy of life of the *Robin Hood* stories. This interpretative power is particularly observable in the portraits of the characters, of Merlin and Vivien and of Arthur. These are splendid in their drawing and intensely meaningful in their character portrayal. The details of the pictures recreate the inner life of the period. They are saturated with the spirit of the age. Together with the exceptional illustrations for *Otto of the Silver Hand*, they established Pyle's reputation as the artist of his time who could best bring to life the medieval period. This in turn brought an overwhelming number of requests that he illustrate writings on the Middle Ages.

Otto of the Silver Hand is the best of his historical fiction, the one which fully reveals the extent of his knowledge of the

Middle Ages, and the only one of Pyle's historical stories to be illustrated in pen and ink. It could not have been illustrated so effectively in any other way. It is a book made beautiful and significant by the delicate harmony, consistently maintained, between the action of the story and the full page illustrations, and between the underlying meanings of the story and the symbolism of the head and tail pieces. It is the book which most closely resembles the work of Dürer; but the illustrations are not so much derivative as they are proof of Pyle's ability to so absorb a period that every detail of a book, writing, decoration, and design, are of that period. Once known, the pictures in this book are unforgettable in their immensely detailed recreation of the life and spirit of the Middle Ages. And once again, they demonstrate that Pyle's theories of illustration are not merely theoretical, but are capable of being put into practice with telling and enriching effect. Excellence of technique is certainly present. But the something more that makes these pictures memorable is the conveyance of the image of the text, the element which he considered so necessary to illustration, if that illustration were to enhance the meaning of the story or content.

Men of Iron, a story of knighthood in England, and *The Story of Jack Ballister's Fortunes*, with its background of the colonial period in America and of piracy, are stories very different from *Otto*. The emphasis is upon action and adventure rather than upon the subtler nuances of the periods. It is a tribute to Pyle's understanding of the requirements of illustration that these books should be illustrated with half tones. The delicacy, intricacy, and refinement of implication of his line drawings would have been so inharmonious with the nature of these stories that mere mention of the fact seems superfluous. The only legitimate purpose in mentioning it is to sharpen the realisation that his tone paintings and his paintings in colour have high merit of their own, in spite of the apparent consensus that his pen drawings constitute his greatest contribution to the art of illustration. The half tones lend to *Men of Iron* and *Jack Ballister* a solid reality, together with an actuality of detail and background eminently suitable to the nature of these stories.

The reasons for the use of half tones in *The Garden Behind the Moon*, an allegory in fairy tale form, is on first thought, less immediately explicable. It cannot be ascribed to a similar desire to achieve reality, since this book is a fantasy. The time of its publication is a possible explanation. Except for the return to line drawings in the Arthurian stories, Pyle at this time was using the medium of painting, in black and white and in colour. However, a knowledge of the book makes it seem more than probable that, once more, his infallible sense of propriety in illustration was chiefly responsible. The allegorical symbolism of *The Garden Behind the Moon* has a note very different from that in his short fairy tales. This note would have been out of tune with the peculiar genius of Pyle's pen and ink illustrations, so much so that one cannot imagine this book illustrated in line. The half tones seem appropriate, even though the unity which distinguishes the earlier books and the later King Arthur volumes has been lost. In spite of this loss, the illustrations in *The Garden Behind the Moon* have beauty of imagination and execution. This is particularly exemplified in two of them, 'He was standing by the open window', on page 69, and 'Fast flew the black winged horse', on page 153.

The volume, variety, and superiority of Pyle's illustrative work had incalculable influence during his lifetime and later. This influence was deepened and extended by the quality of his teaching. The tributes paid him by his students might seem fulsome, sentimental, and too suggestive of hero worship unless attention is directed to the greatest and most creative aspect of his teaching. Given personality, expert knowledge of a subject, fluency, ease, and enthusiasm in presentation on the part of a teacher, and strong interest and motivation on the part of a class, inspiration frequently becomes disturbingly easy and possibly momentary. The greatness of Pyle's teaching lay in the combination of inspiration and challenge—the challenge being provided by the rigorous standards of achievement to which he held his students and which he exemplified in his own work—and the fact that he helped his students to develop their own individuality. None of those who became famous shows a likeness to Pyle in his work. His teaching was intensive and practical, as well as stimulating and idealistic, and its keynote was hard work, and its theme was that there is no easy way to the attainment of the high purposes of creative art. He had also one of the greatest gifts a teacher may possess, that of seeing beneath the first stumbling efforts, the true potentialities of his students, and he spared neither himself nor the student in the development of these potentialities. The tributes which might seem overstated become movingly sincere in the attempt to acknowledge the immensity of the debt owed him not only by those whom he taught but also by future generations. The impressive thing is that the influence emanating from his theories, his work, and his teaching spread from generation to generation and still persists.

III. His Writing for Children

Pyle's best writing for children is in the books in which he did his best illustration. These books are of three kinds, retellings of traditional material, short fairy tales deriving from folk tales, and fiction with an historical background.

His first published writing for children was in the form of brief fables and fairy tales appearing in magazines. His first and last published books for children were retellings of traditional material. Pyle was not the only one in the late nineteenth and early twentieth centuries interested in folk literature and the possibilities of introducing it to children through suitable adaptations. Nathaniel Hawthorne's *A Wonder Book for Boys and Girls* and his *Tanglewood Tales* had been published in the 1850s, as had Charles Kingsley's *The Heroes*. Alfred Church's retellings of the Greek and other epic materials were written in the 1890s and early 1900s. Two of James Baldwin's retellings, *The Story of Siegfried* and *The Story of the Golden Age*, were illustrated by Pyle. Joel Chandler Harris was retelling the Uncle Remus stories, which were accompanied by illustrations by Pyle's friend, A. B. Frost. Andrew Lang and Joseph Jacobs were making their collections of folk tales in the '80s and '90s. The spirit of romanticism in the literature of the time sharpened the interest in folk literature generated many years earlier by the introduction of the Grimms' fairy tales to the English-speaking world. Pyle's temperamental and life-long affinity with folk literature was in tune with the spirit of the time, which produced some classics in retellings of traditional material.

Among these is *The Merry Adventures of Robin Hood*. In this book Pyle has exemplified in full degree the requirements necessary in a reteller and a retelling, if that retelling is to recreate, literally or freely, the spirit and quality of the original. He steeped himself in the original sources of the Robin Hood stories, the old ballads. He became thoroughly conversant with every detail of the story, with every character, with every setting. He was filled with the feeling of the stories, with their love of action and adventure, their jollity and wit, their zest for life, their robust pleasure in food and drink and the fellowship of good comrades, their settings of forest and countryside.

In his retelling, these innate qualities are made emphatic by a prose style so harmonious with the distinctive attributes of the stories as to seem the inevitable expression of their dominant characteristics. The slightly archaic flavour of the language is artless in its ease and spontaneity, utterly without the pretentious, synthetic quality so often present in adaptations of the manner of speech of an earlier era. The animation of the stories is in part due to this touch of the archaic, and is intensified by the sharply delineated physical descriptions and character portrayals of Robin Hood and his men, each of them strongly individualised, and all of them quickened into life by Pyle's lively interpretation of their basic characteristics. A host of other characters, knights and yeomen, noblemen and peasants, beggars, landlords of inns and taverns, priests and burghers, pass through the stories, giving them a sense of teeming life, and a vigorous recreation of the age in which the stories originated. The constant action and adventure take place against a backdrop of scene and setting made beautiful by Pyle's lovely gift of painting word pictures as striking and unforgettable as are his pictures created by pen or brush. The descriptions of forest and countryside, of roads and inns and taverns, of the seasons of the year are so integral a part of the stories that mood and action, all the eager spirit of the tales, seem to be inspired and motivated by setting and situation. It is a book filled with laughter and with merriment, and with youthful relish of the savour of life. Pyle was a young man, thirty years old, when the book was published in 1883.

Nineteen years later, in a letter to Scribners, he suggested that he retell the adventures of King Arthur and his knights, using a style similar to that of Robin Hood, but, in Pyle's words, with a more mature and poetic finish. The task he faced here was far more colossal than that presented by the retelling of the Robin Hood ballads. The material itself is complex, cycle upon cycle of story, intertwined with one another, and all converging upon the central cycle of Arthur himself. The sources are manifold. It is certain that Pyle knew Malory's *Morte d' Arthur*. The comprehensiveness of the four volumes of his retelling, the identities of the stories included, even the manner of retelling, indicate that he consulted other sources but it is not possible to ascertain what these sources were. In a letter to a friend, he speaks of 'the most universally accepted sources' of the King Arthur romances, with a clear implication that he has consulted them. In addition to the extensive initial work involved in familiarising himself with the original material, he was confronted with the necessity of organising the mass of romances so that the four volumes finally decided upon would represent at least an approach to a consecutive whole. Finally he was now dealing with a kind of traditional material as complex in its mood, emotion, and motivation as in its size and pattern. This last aspect of the medieval romance was a source of anxiety to Pyle, and reveals an attitude in him which establishes him as a link between the past and the future in writing for children. The influence of the didactic school in children's literature which dominated the late eighteenth and early nineteenth centuries was dying hard. Hawthorne's and Kingsley's retellings of the Greek myths show the lingering effects of this school of thought, and indeed, so do many books of later periods. Pyle was troubled by the conflict between his desire to present to children only that which is noble and good, and the fact that medieval romance recognises human weakness even in the noblest characters. In a letter to a friend he mentions this difficulty in specific reference to the character of Sir Gawaine. Pyle admits that violence and treachery and greed and hate were an historic side of the Middle Ages. He also admits his reluctance to present this aspect to children. In *Otto of the Silver Hand*, published fifteen years before the first of the King Arthur volumes, he had shown the uglier side of the Middle Ages, and had done it in such a way as to lend distinction to *Otto*. One can only surmise that his interest in the King Arthur cycles was so entirely directed towards their idealism and spirituality that recognition of their less lofty characteristics was distasteful to him. It is also more than probable that his constant insistence on the need for faithfulness to fact in dealing with history took precedence over everything else in *Otto* since this book is realistic fiction based on history. In defence of his attitude in relation to the *King Arthur*, it should be pointed out that in retellings of epics and romances, faithfulness to the original in point of fact frequently necessitates adaptation in view of considerations exacted by recognition of the immaturity and inexperience of children.

Except for the praise given to the illustrations, the retellings of the Arthur stories received less unanimity of acclaim than had the *Robin Hood*. Some contemporary criticism complained that the strength, sincerity, and conviction of Malory was lost in the diffuseness of Pyle's style. There is an element of truth in this criticism. Pyle's style in these books is characterised by prolific use of words, and by a long, complex sentence structure which rings strangely in ears accustomed to the simple and unadorned grandeur of the *Morte d' Arthur*. In Pyle's style, and in his handling of these stories, there is a Celtic rather than an English touch. For him, the appeal of this literature lay in its mysticism, its symbolism, its aura of magic and enchantment, its apprehension of the mystery of life, its mingling of spiritual and physical adventure, its search for the mystery of human destiny. His instinctive response to these elements was part of his inheritance from his mother, herself a strong mystic. These qualities are precisely those with which the Celtic race imbued their great bardic literature. That his style also partakes of Celtic characteristics may have been a matter of instinct rather than intention, but the Celtic strain is unmistakably present. It is observable in the 'magicalising of nature', a phrase of Matthew Arnold's to describe a distinctively Celtic literary habit. It is present in the use of description of scene to induce mood. It is echoed in the beauty of word sounds, in the lilting cadence of long, balanced sentences, in the stateliness of the prose, in the picturesque phrases, like 'the slanting of the day', in the irresistible temptation to interrupt action to draw word pictures vividly beautiful in their details. The four volumes of Arthurian romance represent the most comprehensive retelling of this great body of literature. In interpretation, style, and illustration they have an harmonious beauty which is unique.

It is a temptation to claim that Pyle was as much at home in the world of the folk tale as were the folk peoples who originated this kind of story. His childhood interest in folk stories had been such as to make it natural that his first writing should have been of this genre. For several years subsequent to the publication of 'Hans Gottenlieb the Fiddler' in an 1877 issue of *St Nicholas*, folk and fairy tales by him appeared in the pages of *St Nicholas* and of *Harper's Young People*. At first, they were retellings or amplifications of skeletons of stories discovered in source books. Gradually he developed facility in creating his own stories, using with expert ease the motifs, character types, ways of thought, and manner of expression of the folk tale.

In 1883, he had the idea of writing little stories in verse form, the verse to be decorated by pen and ink sketches. These were published in various issues of *Harper's Young People*, and Pyle at first intended to collect them in a small book which would be a kind of gift book for children. It was decided, however, to combine them with eight of his folk stories which had been published in *Harper's Young People* and to call the book of combined verse and story *Pepper and Salt or Seasoning for Young Folks*. Two years after the publication of *Pepper and Salt* in 1886, the same idea was used in *The Wonder Clock or Four and Twenty Marvellous Tales, Being One for Each Hour of the Day*. In this book, the verses and the accompanying decorations were the work of Howard Pyle's sister, Katherine Pyle, herself the author of several books for children. Seven years elapsed before the publication of his next and last collection of this kind, *Twilight Land*.

The first two of these collections are superior to the third. Those qualities of storytelling and writing which gave the first two books excellence and Pyle pre-eminence as a teller of the so-called modern fairy tale (an ambiguous term) are lacking or at least diminished in *Twilight Land*. The stories in the last book are less folklike and childlike, less representative of Pyle's masterly control of the structure and expression of the folk tale. It is difficult to decide to what extent the diminution of these traits may be due to the nature of the stories. Most of them seem to stem from Eastern rather than Western sources, which may account for their greater degree of subjectivity and maturity. One interesting feature of this book is the introduction, in which Pyle reveals his wide knowledge of folk-tale sources. The introduction also places the setting and situation in which the stories are told, and this in itself is a provocative, though not basically original, idea. A traveller in Twilight Land comes to an inn, where are gathered Aladdin, Ali Baba, Sindbad, Jack the Giant Killer, Bidpai, St George, the Blacksmith who made Death sit in his apple tree, Boots, and many other of the characters in folk literature. Each one of them tells a story.

This criticism of *Twilight Land* should be taken relatively. The stories here are well told, but the stories in *Pepper and Salt* and *The Wonder Clock* are exceptionally told. These two books offer sufficient and convincing evidence that Pyle could, and did, identify himself with the folk tale. All the structural qualities which make this type of story an outstanding example of the short story form are here ... the beginning which, in a few sentences, gives essentials of setting, situation, and character; the close-knit, clearly motivated plot; the complete and final resolution of the tale. These are objective qualities. More subjective and therefore less easy to recreate, less easy even to imitate, are the manner of speech, the peculiarities of style, the way of thought, the kind of shrewdness and wisdom, the quality of humour, the essence of the characters, in short, that whole flavour of the folk tale which sets it apart from any form of sophisticated literature. Few have been able to comprehend these things, and to reproduce them with Pyle's sincerity, ingenuousness, and thoroughly sympathetic understanding. It is as if he originated these elements, rather than adapted them to his own use. He did add original touches, in the way of picturesque phrase, and gentle admonitions, but these are never disharmonious. He is of his age in his inclination to point a lesson. But in these stories, he seems to yield to the temptation with amusement at his inability to resist. As a result, the morals are accepted by the reader with a similar sense of amusement. It is also true that their phrasing is ingratiating and their relevance to the spirit of the story such that they never seem to be superimposed on the story.

The Garden Behind the Moon is Pyle's only long fairy tale. The origin of the story was in the death of his son, which took place while Pyle and his wife were on vacation in Jamaica, and before they could return home. The theme of the book is the search for the meaning of life and death and of the spiritual nature of man. It is an allegory in which the Moon Angel represents the angel of death, and the garden the place in another life where little children go after death. Inevitably the book has a sad and serious note struck first in the Dedication . . . 'To the Little Boy in the Moon Garden this Book is Dedicated by his Father'. The sadness is restrained and moving, and there is a felt sincerity in the book. Again, the style is notable for the vivid word pictures, those of the garden being touched with nostalgic memories of the beloved garden of his childhood. Pyle's ability to paint a word picture reminds one of the comparable ability Kenneth Grahame shows in *The Wind in the Willows*. One wonders whether Pyle ever knew Grahame's book, which was published three years before Pyle's death. Kenneth Grahame and Howard Pyle might well have been brought together by Theodore Roosevelt, among whose favourite books were *The Merry Adventures of Robin Hood* and *The Wind in the Willows*.

The Garden Behind the Moon has overtones of social consciousness. This is pointedly present in one of the scenes witnessed by the boy David from a window in the moon—a boatload of slaves, fastened together with ropes. David sees the deaths of two of the slaves, a young mother and her baby, and hears the exultant singing of thousands of voices which heralds the entry of mother and child into the garden. In respect of social consciousness, Pyle's fantasy is like some of the great fantasies written during his lifetime, notably Kingsley's *The Water Babies* and George MacDonald's books.

The origin of *The Garden Behind the Moon* which necessarily controls its nature makes comparison with other fantasies of the same period seem somewhat inappropriate. However, except for the reiterated use of certain devices, there is little similarity among the really great fantasies. At the same time, there are certain essentials which should be present in every fantasy. *The Garden Behind the Moon* has a degree of beauty in expression and meaning, in conception and execution, it has a moving pathos and sincerity, but it does not attain the stature of the great fantasies of its time, especially those by English writers of the late nineteenth and early twentieth centuries. It does not have the lingering sense of enchantment of George MacDonald's stories, the charm and variety of mood and emotion of *The Wind in the Willows*, the extraordinary power of creative imagination of W. H. Hudson's *A Little Boy Lost*. It rises above the average, but it does not achieve greatness.

Pyle's three books of historical fiction for children reflect his interest in history and his astonishing grasp of the most minute details of the life of a period. He was particularly interested in the colonial period in America and in the Middle Ages in Europe, and his books with historical background grow out of his particular knowledge of these two periods.

The Story of Jack Ballister's Fortunes has a long subtitle which is representative of the romanticism of the age and of the book and which succeeds in being as good a summary of the content of the story as could be written, 'Being the narrative of the adventures of a young gentleman of good family, who was kidnapped in the year 1719 and carried to the plantations of the continent of Virginia, where he fell in with that famous pirate Captain Edward Teach, or Blackbeard; of his escape from the pirates and the rescue of a young lady from out of their hands.' The introduction to the book tells of the situation which gives rise to the story—the need of the Virginia planters for intelligent labour, the unsuccessful competition with the New England colonies for such labour, the resultant profit in the exportation of labour from England, and the consequent reprehensible habit of kidnapping men and women from England to meet the demand. This background, together with the introduction of one of Pyle's favourite pirates, Blackbeard, inevitably means that the emphasis in the story is on adventure. The assets of the book are its well constructed plot, the plentiful action, and the authentic portrayal of Colonial America. To the adult interested in Pyle as a person, there is also the charm of the reflection of Pyle's childhood in Jack Ballister's memory of his mother and in his recollection of the garden of his boyhood home. The description of the garden is reminiscent of the garden described in Pyle's autobiographical sketch in *The Woman's Home Companion*. The positive qualities of the story are somewhat mitigated by a few negative ones. The progress of the plot, which is essentially a good one, is hindered by the interruptions provoked by Pyle's inclination to use opportunities afforded by the story to point lessons.

The morals here are digressions, superimposed on the text, not an inherent part of it as they are in the fairy tale collections, in *King Arthur*, and in *Otto*. Neither does the dialogue have the spontaneity characteristic of these other books.

Men of Iron, laid in England in the fifteenth century, suffers a little from the same faults. Nevertheless, it too has good points. It is also a story of strong adventure in which the unifying thread is the character of the boy Myles Falworth, and the chief motivation Myles' intention to redeem his father's good name and estate in life, lost because of his support of Richard II. Myles is a life-like boy in his love of physical exploit, in his impulsiveness, and in his rebellion against what is to him unjust authority. To children, one of the most appealing features of the book would be Pyle's capture of the delight boys take in secret hiding places. For children interested in the institution of chivalry there is also the fascination of the descriptions of the training necessary for knighthood. As a whole, *Men of Iron*, with its more single-minded concentration on a direct plot and its greater simplicity, is a more genuine children's book than *The Story of Jack Ballister's Fortunes*, which is closer to the interests of the adolescent.

Again, his first book in this field of writing, *Otto of the Silver Hand*, is superior. In its own and different way, it offers an interpretation of medieval Germany as live and sensitive as the interpretation of Shakespearian England in John Bennett's *Master Skylark*, published nine years after *Otto*. Here Pyle's scruples as to the susceptibilities of children did not prevent him from revealing some of the harshness of life in the Middle Ages, its ugliness as well as its beauty, and the result is a great book. It is also proof that children in their reading may be confronted with evil as well as good, so long as the presentation is made understandable by the quality of compassion which Pyle displays in *Otto*. The story in all its aspects, character, incident, and emotion, is constructed on the principle of contrast, good opposed to evil, savagery to gentleness, love to hate, greed to self-sacrifice, physical victory to spiritual victory. Through it moves the figure of Otto, seemingly a victim of the worst passions of the period, actually a symbol of hope for the future. It is a gentle, tender, moving story. It is fitting to re-emphasise the fact that the spirit of compassionate understanding which permeates the book is a rare quality in books for children or books for adults.

In children's book collections in the United States are three other books which are compilations of Pyle's writings and illustrations. *Stolen Treasure*, published in 1907, contains four pirate stories: *With the Buccaneers*; *Tom Chist and the Treasure Box*; *The Ghost of Captain Brand*; *The Devil at New Hope*. These were previously published in adult periodicals. *Howard Pyle's Book of Pirates*, published by Harper's in 1921, is a collection of his writings on pirates with a selection of his best pirate illustrations. The success of this compilation led the compiler, Merle Johnson, to collect from books and magazines a large number of Pyle's historical illustrations. This collection was published in 1923, also by Harper's, with the title *Howard Pyle's Book of the American Spirit*. The text is taken from original sources, with a large degree of editing by Francis J. Dowd. These two books are splendid examples of Pyle's illustrations of pirates and of historical subjects.

IV. His Other Work

The quality and amount of Pyle's writing and illustrating of children's books reasonably could constitute the work of a lifetime. In addition to his work for children, he wrote novels and short stories for adults; he illustrated more than one hundred books by other authors; and his illustrations appeared with amazing frequency in many of the most outstanding periodicals of the day.

Except for *Rejected of Men*, his novels are strongly reflective of his predilection for adventure and romance. The first, *Within the Capes*, published in 1885, is a sea story which contains, incidentally, a fine description of a Friends' meeting. Robert Louis Stevenson praised the quality of adventure in *A Modern Aladdin*, a story of a French boy claimed as a nephew by the Comte de St Germaine. However, Stevenson, who considered that romantic adventure is amoral, a thesis well supported in his essay *A Gossip on Romance*, vigorously deplored the moral tacked on to the end of the book.

The best of Pyle's adult novels and short stories came from his interest in pirates; the most fantastically romantic, from his love of adventure and romance; and the most provocative, from his habit of religious and philosophical speculation.

The first result of his interest in pirates was *The Rose of Paradise*, in which the pirate, Edward England, is a prominent and well portrayed character. It is a good story, which uses the technique of first-person narrative effectively, and which has a fair degree of action, suspense and drama. His second pirate novel, *The Ruby of Kishmoor*, was not published until 1908, though it had been written many years earlier. It is the story of a young Quaker who meets with extraordinary adventures on a trip to Jamaica. There is a strong contrast, almost humorous, between the Quaker's rather prosaic and down-to-earth character and the high degree of adventure which befell him.

Among his best writing in pirate lore are the four stories which were ultimately published as the book *Stolen Treasure*. Of these stories, listed in the previous chapter, 'Captain Brand' is particularly good, and unusually interesting because of the touch of fantasy introduced.

His interest in pirates led to interest in rogues in general, which in turn produced articles on such rogues as Claude du Val, Jack Sheppard, Jonathan Wild and others. The material for these accounts was drawn largely from chapbook literature.

The subtitle for another of his novels, *The Price of Blood*, describes the book as 'An Extravaganza of New York Life in 1807'. Extravaganza it certainly is; today it would be called a thriller, and a thoroughgoing one at that. It is peopled with mysterious and dangerous characters from the East, who pursue and kill, by the most extraordinary means, two brothers who manoeuvred a political revolution in the Orient, and escaped with a treasure. One suspects that Pyle wrote it with tongue in cheek, indulging to the utmost and in fun, his love of mystery and romance.

Rejected of Men in its day must have been a startling book. It transfers the time of Christ to contemporary America and tells the story of Christ from the point of view of the Pharisees, Levites, and others who opposed His teaching. Its origin was undoubtedly in Pyle's habit of speculative religious thought which is also evidenced in a long and interesting correspondence with William Dean Howells on the subject of religious faith. The thesis of the book is that he who threatens the existing order of society and religion will always be destroyed by the Pharisees of the day, who are born to crucify the truth, as they did nineteen hundred years ago. From their point of view, it is better that one man should die, than that the established order should be overthrown. The story opens with the preaching of John the Baptist, his appeal to the masses, and the consternation into which he threw Church and society.

This book was refused by several publishers, on the grounds that readers would object to the contemporary recreation of the time of Christ, and to the point of view from which the teaching and ministry of Christ is presented. At last it was accepted and published by Harper's. The publication was followed by the anticipated objections. But there were also some readers who felt that its theme was important, and that the book demonstrated the theme effectively and dramatically.

Howard Pyle was both romanticist and realist, and these seemingly opposed traits became, in him, complementary. This is clearly evident in his illustrations for adult material, not only in fact, but also in his attitudes towards his illustrations.

In the early 1900s, there were two dominating, and sometimes conflicting interests in literature, interest in the romantic and interest in the realistic. The romantic interest found one outlet in medievalism and in stories of the Middle Ages. It is noteworthy that Pyle's reputation as an authority on the Middle Ages was based initially on the illustrations in his children's books concerned with that period. Early in the 1900s he painted in colour a series of pictures which were published in *Harper's Maga-*

zine, many of them as illustrations for James Branch Cabell's medieval stories. These were so successful, so immensely popular, that the pressure on him for this kind of illustration became very great. One cannot wonder at the wide appeal of these pictures. Their colours are lovely, their spirit romantic, and their composition excellent. Pyle himself distrusted the response to his pictures, feeling that the undoubted popular interest in medievalism was being nurtured by stories which he considered artificial. He believed that much of this writing fell between history and fantasy and was true to neither type. He disliked being associated with this kind of writing and felt that his work was adversely affected by the stilted and conventionalized quality of his illustrations. This quality is observable, and is probably due partly to the nature of the stories illustrated and partly to too great a concentration on this one type of illustration. There was, therefore, some justification for this feeling and for his reluctance to spend so much of his time and artistic endeavour on this one kind of picture. And yet, as one looks at the best of these, the ones used to illustrate James Branch Cabell's stories, and particularly those for Mark Twain's article on Joan of Arc, published in *Harper's Magazine* for December, 1904, one cannot help but be glad Pyle did them. The four illustrations for Mark Twain's article, published as a book in 1919, are unusually fine and definitely deserving of the praise given them. One is an arresting portrait of Joan of Arc in full armour. 'The Triumphal Entry into Rheims' is exciting in its drama, and beautiful in its colour, while 'Guarded by Rough English Soldiers' has a touching, moving quality. Mark Twain was evidently right when he insisted that for this article, Pyle was the only possible illustrator. Comparison of these pictures with those for *The Lady of Shalott*, published in

1881, and one of the first books Pyle illustrated, proves the tremendous advance made in reproduction of colour in the years between the 1880s and the 1900s, as well as in Pyle's own technique. He is said to have looked back on *The Lady of Shalott* with horror, and it is diffuse and elaborate in comparison with the fine simplicity and meaningful details of his later work.

He was much happier with his pirate illustrations. The publication of *The Rose of Paradise* led Harper's to ask Pyle to write an illustrated article on the ancient strongholds of pirates in the West Indies. This article, *Buccaneers and Marooners of the Spanish Main*, was published in *Harper's Monthly* for August 1877. The illustrations for this article are very fine, as are those for a later article, *The Fate of a Treasure Town*, published in the same magazine in 1905. They are dramatic, romantic, striking in their colour. The majority of his pirate pictures, and there are many, are magnificent, strong in character portrayal, imaginative in story-telling quality, vigorous, forceful, and compelling. One look at some of the originals, hung in the Delaware Art Center in Wilmington, shows that the reproductions, impressive as they are, do not do justice to the scope of the pictures, to the intense colour, to the fineness of detail, to the entire conceptions of the pictures. One look is unsatisfactory; to many of them, the viewer is drawn a second and a third time, and it is difficult to select those which most deserve comment. Possibly the one which most captures the imagination is 'Marooned'. The caption for this original painting in the Delaware Art Center says that it was never reproduced but that a very similar picture illustrated 'Buccaneers and Marooners of America'. This illustration is one of those most frequently mentioned in comment upon his pirate pictures. Both the painting in the Art Center and the illustration are poignant in their depiction of dejection and despair. Pyle's biographer, Charles D. Abbott, says that the whole meaning of the picture is expressed in the pirate's hands, and this is very true. Hanging loosely clasped, as the pirate sits on the lonely beach, his head bowed, the hands are the embodiment of resigned surrender to fate.

No less excellent in their own field are his pictures dealing with American history. The vast extent of his research and the resultant detailed knowledge produced so many illustrations in this subject that it is impossible to discuss these illustrations comprehensively. It has been necessary to select a few examples, the selection being governed by the representative quality of the illustrations and by their importance.

In 1895, Woodrow Wilson, then at Princeton University, wrote a series of articles on George Washington for *Harper's Monthly*. Wilson was insistent that Pyle should illustrate the series. The consensus of opinion was that the illustrations Pyle did for these articles were the most notable that had appeared in American periodicals. Their notability lay chiefly in their technical excellence and the expert knowledge of the period revealed in them. Wilson so admired them that he asked the publishers for proof copies to be framed for his study. Such was Pyle's knowledge of the subject that he did not hesitate to question some of Wilson's facts, and Wilson, a true scholar, welcomed such questioning. These pictures, after being exhibited in Boston, were bought by a group of prominent men for the Public Library in that city.

The illustrations done for Senator Henry Cabot Lodge's *Story of the Revolution* are intensely interesting. Much planning and research went into the making of these pictures. They were done originally in colour, but the colour was not reproduced in the publication in magazine or in book form. There had been a suggestion that eventually they should be hung in the Library of Congress, but apparently some regulation governing ownership of pictures hung in government buildings prevented this. Several of these pictures were sold, but the one entitled 'Clark on His Way to Kankaskia' was given by Pyle to Lodge. Senator Lodge later gave it to President Theodore Roosevelt, who greatly admired it. A large part of the interest aroused by the pictures is due to the notes which accompany many of them. These notes not only briefly describe the occasion of the pictures, but also identify such things as characters, officers, regiments, ships of war, details of battles, circumstances with which the pictures deal. They are ample and fascinating evidence of Pyle's immense knowledge of history.

His strong sense of history gave him a feeling for time and place as shown by his illustrations for such period fiction as Margaret Deland's *Old Chester Tales* and, more delightfully, for Oliver Wendell Holmes' poem *The One Hoss Shay*. The pen and ink sketches for this and for Holmes' other poem, *Dorothy Q.*, not only portrays the setting and incidents of the poems, but also enhance the humour deliciously.

Recognition of Pyle's ability to capture both actuality and atmosphere of time and place led Dr S. Weir Mitchell to insist that Pyle must illustrate his novel, *Hugh Wynne, Free Quaker*. Pyle was reluctant to accept this commission, and his letters to the author and to the publisher indicate how much trouble and dissatisfaction this work caused him. He wanted to please Dr Mitchell, a man of strong opinions, but at the same time, he did not feel that his particular kind of historical picture-making lent itself to the illustration of stories. In my childhood, this was my favourite historical novel. In the years since, any mention of the book, or any association with it, has brought an immediate mental vision of the illustrations in complete detail. This would seem to imply that they are far better, and far more imaginatively illustrative of the stories than Pyle apparently thought they were.

Although they cannot be related to his medieval, pirate, and historical pictures, the decorations for Edwin Markham's collection of poems, *Man With a Hoe*, deserve mention. These poems are finely illustrated in pen and ink, and the strength of line, the symbolic quality of the sketches, are reminiscent of the beauty of his work in *Otto of the Silver Hand*.

Had Pyle lived to return from Europe, it is probable that he might have devoted a large amount of time and attention to mural painting. Judging from the success of the few murals painted before his death, it is equally probable that he would have attained eminence in this kind of art. 'The Battle of Monmouth' in the State Capitol of Minnesota, 'The Landing of Carteret' in the Essex County Court House in Newark, New Jersey, and in the Hudson County Court House, Jersey City, New Jersey, the five pictures concerned with the discovery of the Hudson River and the early settlements there (he was assisted in the finishing of these last pictures by Stanley Arthur and Frank Schoonover) won such praise that it is justifiable to assume that many more such commissions would have been offered him.

v. Conclusion

In the slightly more than thirty years which constituted Howard Pyle's productive lifetime, he created a body of illustration and writing which made him pre-eminent in his time and for all time. By reason of his distinctive qualities as an illustrator, he was the outstanding figure in a group of artists who, with the coming of the twentieth century, had brought to the art of illustration a high degree of excellence. His distinctive qualities as an illustrator are so many and so meaningful that one hesitates to enumerate them, lest the enumeration bring the accusation of extravagance and exaggeration. Nevertheless a fair and adequate appraisal of his place and influence in illustration demands emphasis on those aspects of his genius which contributed most to the permanence of his work and the extent of his influence. His originality of conception and execution is rooted in strength of creative imagination, which led him always to concentrate on the inner meaning of whatever he was illustrating. His power of imagination and his search for significance inevitably produced a dislike of regimentation, a distrust of insistence upon prescribed techniques and styles. His understanding of what can be conveyed by a union of the written and pictorial arts was unique in his day, and not surpassed since his day. His sense of total book design is infallible, and he set an example in this respect which remains an inspiration. He was an idealist, unsatisfied with anything less than the attainment of excellence. He was at the same time a realist, but a creative realist, who could insist on the fundamental need for accuracy of detail, and at the same time avoid the pedantry and tyranny of meaningless detail. His versatility in subject and medium had no tinge of superficiality, something not in his nature. His understanding of and devotion to the art of illustration made him, in theory and performance, a prophet of the future. His influence on illustration is permanent, not only because of his own high achievement, but also because of the power of his teaching, which has been transmitted by those who studied under him to succeeding generations of artists.

The writing for which he is and will be remembered is in the field of children's books. This is as it should be, for he came to love best his writing for children, and none knew better than he that a book for a child, beloved by generations of children, is assured of eternal life, and that the author of such a book is one who has given to mankind a gift of lasting value. Books of beauty and excellence, of wholesomeness and sanity, of joy and humour and pathos, of imagination and constructive realism read in childhood leave an ineradicable impression. High praise is rightly given to him who has written a genuine classic for children, a classic in the sense of a book which conveys something worth conveying, which has appealed to enough children over enough time to ensure its universality. Among such classics are Howard Pyle's *The Merry Adventures of Robin Hood*, *Pepper and Salt*, *The Wonder Clock*, *Otto of the Silver Hand*, and the four books of the Arthurian cycles, books made beautiful by Pyle's two-fold genius as author-illustrator.

Skilled craftsman in the graphic and written arts, romanticist and realist, lover of a good story and devotee of truth, man of spirituality and integrity, inspired and challenging teacher, he is the first truly great American author and illustrator of children's books.

BIBLIOGRAPHY

Bibliography

The majority of the books written and/or illustrated by Howard Pyle were first published in periodicals. The dates of publication in the bibliographies are the dates of book publication; an asterisk indicates that the book is still in print.

I. CHILDREN'S BOOKS WRITTEN AND ILLUSTRATED BY HOWARD PYLE

*The Merry Adventures of Robin Hood of Great Renown in Nottinghamshire. New York, Charles Scribner's Sons, 1883

*Pepper and Salt or Seasoning for Young Folks. New York, Harper and Brothers, 1886

*The Wonder Clock or Four and Twenty Marvellous Tales, Being One For Each Hour of The Day. Embellished With Verses by Katherine Pyle. New York, Harper and Brothers, 1888

*Otto of the Silver Hand. New York, Charles Scribner's Sons, 1888

*Men of Iron. New York, Harper and Brothers, 1892

The Story of Jack Ballister's Fortunes. Being the narrative of the adventures of a young gentleman of good family, who was kidnapped in the year of 1719, and carried to the plantations of the continent of Virginia, where he fell in with that famous Pirate Captain Edward Teach, or Blackbeard; of his escape from the pirates and the rescue of a young lady from out of their hands. New York, The Century Company, 1895

The Garden Behind the Moon; A Real Story of the Moon Angel. New York, Charles Scribner's Sons, 1895

Twilight Land. New York, Harper and Brothers, 1895

*Some Merry Adventures of Robin Hood of Great Renown in Nottinghamshire. New York, Charles Scribner's Sons, 1902. (An abridged edition of The Merry Adventures of Robin Hood published by Charles Scribner's Sons in 1883)

213

The Story of King Arthur and His Knights. New York, Charles
   Scribner's Sons, 1903
The Story of The Champions of The Round Table. New York,
   Charles Scribner's Sons, 1905
The Story of Sir Launcelot and His Companions. New York,
   Charles Scribner's Sons, 1907
The Story of the Grail and the Passing of Arthur. New York,
   Charles Scribner's Sons, 1910

II. COLLECTIONS OF HIS WRITING AND ILLUSTRATIONS

Stolen Treasure, New York, Harper and Brothers, 1907. (Contains
   four stories previously published in *Harper's Round Table* and
   Harper's Weekly : 'With the Buccaneers', *Harper's Round Table*,
   June 29, 1897; 'Tom Chist and the Treasure Box', *Harper's
   Round Table*, March 24, 1896; 'The Ghost of Captain Brand',
   Harper's Weekly, December 19, 1896; 'The Devil at New Hope',
   Harper's Weekly, December 18, 1897)
*The Book of Laughter. Selections from Bret Harte, Howard Pyle,
   Joel Chandler Harris, John Habberton, Frank R. Stockton and
   Others.* Edited by Katherine N. Birdsall and George Haven
   Putnam. New York, G. P. Putnam's Sons, 1911. (Contains
   three stories by Howard Pyle, the earliest of his writings.
   'Hans Gottenlieb the Fiddler', *St Nicholas*, April, 1877; 'Drum-
   mer Fritz and his Exploits', *St Nicholas*, September, 1877;
   'Robin Goodfellow and his Friend Bluetree', *St Nicholas*, June,
   1879)
*Howard Pyle's Book of Pirates; Fiction, Fact and Fancy Con-
   cerning the Buccaneers and Marooners of the Spanish Main;
   from the Writings and Pictures of Howard Pyle.* Compiled by
   Merle Johnson, New York, Harper and Brothers, 1921
*Howard Pyle's Book of the American Spirit; The Romance of
   American History, Pictured by Howard Pyle.* Compiled by
   Merle Johnson, with narrative descriptive text from original
   sources, edited by Francis J. Dowd. New York, Harper and
   Brothers, 1923

BIBLIOGRAPHY

III. ENGLISH EDITIONS

The Merry Adventures of Robin Hood of Great Renown in Notting-hamshire. London, Sampson Low, Marston, Searle, and Rivington, 1883

†*The Wonder Clock or Four and Twenty Marvellous Tales, Being One For Each Hour of The Day*. London, Osgood McIlvane and Company, 1888

†*Otto of the Silver Hand*. London, Sampson Low, Marston, Searle, and Rivington, 1888

Men of Iron. London, Osgood McIlvane and Company, 1892

The Story of Jack Ballister's Fortunes. London, Osgood McIlvane and Company, 1897

The Garden Behind the Moon. London, Laurence Bullen, 1895

Twilight Land. London, Osgood McIlvane and Company, 1895

†*The Story of King Arthur and His Knights*. London, George Newnes Ltd, 1903

The Story of The Champions of The Round Table. London, George Newnes Ltd, 1905

The Story of Sir Launcelot and His Companions. London, Chapman and Hall, 1907

The Story of the Grail and the Passing of Arthur. London, Bickers and Son, 1910

† These titles are available in Dover paperback editions, distributed in Great Britain by Constable and Company Ltd

IV. ADULT NOVELS WRITTEN BY PYLE

Within the Capes. New York, Charles Scribner's Sons. 1885

The Rose of Paradise, being a detailed account of certain adventures that happened to Captain John Mackra in connection with the famous Pirate, Edward England, in the year 1720, off the Island of Juanna in the Mozambique Channel; writ by himself and now for the first time published. New York, Harper and Brothers, 1888

A Modern Aladdin or, The Wonderful Adventures of Oliver Munier. An Extravaganza in Four Acts. New York, Harper and Brothers, 1892

The Price of Blood. An Extravaganza of New York Life in 1807. Boston, Richard G. Badger and Company, 1899

Rejected of Men. A Story of To-day. New York, Harper and
Brothers, 1903
The Ruby of Kishmoor. New York, Harper and Brothers, 1908

V. A SELECTIVE LIST OF BOOKS WRITTEN BY OTHERS AND ILLUSTRATED BY PYLE

The Lady of Shalott, by Alfred Lord Tennyson. New York, Dodd,
Mead and Company, 1881
The Story of Siegfried, by James Baldwin. New York, Charles
Scribner's Sons, 1882
A Story of The Golden Age, by James Baldwin. New York,
Charles Scribner's Sons, 1887
The One Hoss Shay with Its Companion Poems, by Oliver Wendell
Holmes. Boston and New York, Houghton Mifflin and
Company, 1892
*Dorothy Q. Together with a ballad of The Boston Tea Party and
Grandmother's Story of Bunker Hill Battle*, by Oliver Wendell
Holmes. Boston and New York, Houghton Mifflin and
Company, 1893
The Autocrat of The Breakfast Table, by Oliver Wendell Holmes.
Boston and New York, Houghton Mifflin and Company, 1894
George Washington, by Woodrow Wilson. New York, Harper and
Brothers, 1896
Hugh Wynne, Free Quaker, by S. Weir Mitchell, M. D. New
York, The Century Company, 1897
The Story of The Revolution, by Henry Cabot Lodge. New York,
Charles Scribner's Sons, 1898
Old Chester Tales, by Margaret Deland. New York, Harper and
Brothers, 1899
The Man with the Hoe and Other Poems, by Edwin Markham.
New York, Doubleday McClure Company, 1900
The Line of Love, by James Branch Cabell. New York, Harper and
Brothers, 1905
Chivalry, by James Branch Cabell. New York, Harper and
Brothers, 1909
The Soul of Melicent, by James Branch Cabell. New York,
Frederick A. Stokes Company, 1813

BIBLIOGRAPHY

Saint Joan of Arc, by Mark Twain. New York, Harper and
Brothers, 1919

VI. PERIODICALS IN WHICH PYLE'S WRITINGS AND ILLUSTRATIONS APPEARED

Scribner's Monthly, 1876-1878
St Nicholas, 1877-1903
Harper's Weekly, 1877-1907
Harper's New Monthly Magazine, 1878-1900
Harper's Young People, 1880-1894
Harper's Bazaar, 1882-1891
Scribner's Magazine, 1887-1903
The Century Magazine, 1893-1902
Harper's Round Table, 1896-1897
Collier's Weekly, 1898-1906
Harper's Monthly Magazine, 1901-1912

VII. MURAL PAINTINGS BY PYLE

The Battle of Nashville. State Capitol, Minnesota, 1906
The Landing of Carteret. Essex County Court House, Newark,
New Jersey, 1907
*Hendryk Hudson and the Half-Moon—Peter Stuyvesant and the
English Fleet—Life in an Old Dutch Town—Dutch Soldier—
English Soldier*. Hudson County Court House, Jersey City,
New Jersey, 1910

VIII. COLLECTIONS OF HOWARD PYLE MATERIALS

The Howard Pyle Collection. Delaware Art Center, Wilmington,
Delaware
The Thornton Oakley Collection of Howard Pyle Materials.
Rare Book Department, Free Library of Philadelphia, Phila-
delphia, Pennsylvania

IX. BIBLIOGRAPHY OF HIS WRITINGS
AND ILLUSTRATIONS

Howard Pyle : A Record of His Illustrations and Writings. The Wilmington Society of Fine Arts. Compiled by Willard S. Morse and Gertrude Brinckle. Wilmington, Delaware, 1921

X. WRITINGS ABOUT HOWARD PYLE

Pen Drawing and Pen Draughtsmen : Their Work and Their Methods, a Study of the Art today with Technical Suggestions, by Joseph Pennell. London and New York, Macmillan and Company, 1889

The House of Harper : A Century of Publishing in Franklin Square, by Joseph Henry Harper. New York, Harper and Brothers, 1912

When I was a Little Boy, by Howard Pyle. In *The Woman's Home Companion,* volume 39, April, 1912

Howard Pyle, Maker of Pictures and Stories, by Hildegarde Hawthorne. In *St Nicholas,* volume 42, May-October, 1915

American Graphic Art, by Frank Weitenkampf. New York, Macmillan, 1924

Howard Pyle, a Chronicle ; with an Introduction by N. C. Wyeth and Many Illustrations from Howard Pyle's Works, by Charles D. Abbott. New York, Harper and Brothers, 1925

Howard Pyle, A Backward Glance, by Virginia Kirkus. In *The Horn Book Magazine,* volume 5, November, 1929

Out of The Dark Ages, by Eric Kelly. In *The Three Owls, Third Book,* by Anne Carroll Moore. New York, Coward-McCann, 1931

The Illustrated Book, by Frank Weitenkampf. Cambridge, The Harvard University Press.

Children's Classics, by Alice M. Jordan. In *The Horn Book Magazine,* volume 23, July-August, 1947

Howard Pyle and His Times, by Robert Lawson. In *Illustrators of Children's Books, 1744-1945,* by Bertha E. Mahony, Louise P. Latimer, and Beulah Folmsbee. Boston, The Horn Book, 1947

Howard Pyle, Teacher of Illustration, by Richard Wayne Lykes. Unpublished thesis, Philadelphia Graduate School of Arts and Sciences, The University of Pennsylvania, 1947

From Rollo to Tom Sawyer, by Alice M. Jordan. Boston, The Horn Book, 1948

The Book in America : A History of the Making and Selling of Books in the United States, by Hellmut Lehmann-Haupt. New York, R. R. Bowker Company, 1951

Howard Pyle, His Art and Personality, by Thornton Oakley. An address given on November 8, 1951, at the Free Library of Philadelphia, with an introduction by Joseph Carson, President, Board of Trustees, on the occasion of Thornton Oakley's presentation of his collection of Howard Pyle materials to the Free Library of Philadelphia. Privately printed, 1951

Howard Pyle, His Contribution to Children's Literature, by Jean R. Russell. Unpublished thesis, Pittsburgh, Carnegie Institute of Technology, Carnegie Library School, 1952

The Influence of Howard Pyle on American Illustration, by Ruth G. Patterson. Unpublished thesis, Cleveland, Graduate School of Library Science, Western Reserve University, 1954

Illustrating Children's Books—History, Technique, Production, by Henry C. Pitz. New York, Watson-Guptill Publications, 1963